WINDOWS 2000 PROFESSIONAL
in easy steps

MICHAEL PRICE

COMPUTER
STEP

In easy steps is an imprint of Computer Step
Southfield Road . Southam
Warwickshire CV47 OFB . England

http://www.ineasysteps.com

Notice of Liability

Every effort has been made to ensure that this book contains accurate
and current information. However, Computer Step and the author shall
not be liable for any loss or damage suffered by readers as a result of
any information contained herein.

Trademarks

Microsoft® and Windows® are registered trademarks of Microsoft
Corporation. All other trademarks are acknowledged as belonging to
their respective companies.

Printed and bound in the United Kingdom

ISBN 1-84078-202-1

Contents

1 Installing Windows 2000   7

Windows 2000 family   8
Windows 2000 Professional   10
Windows 2000 licences   12
Requirements   13
Methods of installing   14
New installation   15
The setup process   16
GUI setup   17
Administration   18
Setup from CD   19
Upgrading your PC   20
The upgraded system   22
Retaining the old system   23

2 Exploring Windows 2000   25

Initial tasks   26
Desktop items   27
My Computer folders   28
Start menu   30
Search assistance   31
Recent Documents   32
Program groups   33
Starting programs   34
Additional components   36
Taskbar and toolbars   37
Closing down   38
Explorer view   39
Files and folders   40
Context menu   42
Send To   43
Registered file types   44

3

Windows Components   45

Control Panel options   46
Add/remove   48
Date/time   50
Display   51
Fonts   52
Keyboard   53
Mouse   54
Start menu accessories   55
Calculator   56
Command Prompt   57
Imaging   58
Notepad   59
Paint   60
WordPad   61
Entertainment   62
Games   64
Windows Explorer   66

4

Accessing the Internet   67

Internet Connection Wizard   68
Choosing your ISP   70
Manual setup   71
Internet over LAN   73
Set up Internet mail   74
Completing the definition   76
Connecting   77
Dial-up status   78
Internet Explorer   80
Home page   81
Internet Connection Sharing   82
Enabling ICS   83
IP addressing   84
ICS in action   85
LAN status   86

5 Installing Applications   87

Certified for Windows	88
Methods of installing	90
Application migration	91
Paint Shop Pro	92
Visio	94
Installing via Run	96
Compressed applications	97
What to watch for	98
Adding/removing programs	100
Legacy applications	102
MS-DOS applications	103
Managing the Start menu	104

6 Customising the Layout   105

Default Desktop	106
Tile wallpaper	108
Active Desktop	109
Colour and resolution	110
Appearance	112
Screensavers	114
Changing frequency	116
Other options	117
Start menu and Taskbar	118
Adding My Computer	120
Customising the Taskbar	121
Taskbar toolbars	122
Other customisations	124

7 Exchanging Information   125

Sharing information	126
Using the Clipboard	127
Viewing the ClipBook	128
Pasting text	130
Text to Paint	132
Cut and paste images	133
Add images to text	134
Paste to Notepad	136
Cut and Paste	137
Drag-and-drop	138

Clip from Command Prompt   139
Embedded objects   140
Linking objects   142
OLE Registration   144

Controlling the Printer   145

8

Windows printers   146
Adding printers   147
Manual install   148
Printer properties   150
Network printers   152
Driver verification   154
Application printing   155
Creating a print queue   156
Document printing   158
Generic text printers   160
Print and hold   162
Many printers in one   163
Replacing printers   164

Networking Windows 2000   165

9

PC networks   166
Server-based LANs   168
Peer-to-peer LANs   169
Planning the network structure   170
Getting help with the design   172
Higher speeds   174
Adapter cards   175
Network setup   176
Sharing devices   178
Browsing the network   180
Mapping drives and folders   182
Connecting two PCs   184
Windows Update   185

Index   187

Installing Windows 2000

This chapter looks at the Windows 2000 family, and at the process of installing Windows 2000 from the CD-ROM as a fresh system, as an upgrade from Windows 98 or NT 4 or as a dual-boot system (retaining the original operating system).

Covers

Windows 2000 family | 8

Windows 2000 Professional | 10

Windows 2000 licences | 12

Requirements | 13

Methods of installing | 14

New installation | 15

The setup process | 16

GUI setup | 17

Administration | 18

Setup from CD | 19

Upgrading your PC | 20

The upgraded system | 22

Retaining the old system | 23

Chapter One

Windows 2000 family

Windows 2000 is the operating system of choice for business workstations/network servers. To achieve this range of support, Windows 2000 has been packaged into a family of four products.

Windows 2000 Professional

This is the typical use for a home office or small business environment, and forms the main scenario for this book.

This is the operating system for business PCs, desktops and mobiles. It can be used on a stand-alone system, as you might previously have used Windows 98, to run user applications or games. It is also used for a group of PCs in a peer to peer network or across the Internet. A PC running the Professional edition can act as a server, share files, printers and Internet connections with other PCs, and optionally act as a user (client) workstation at the same time. All the software required is already included.

Finally, Windows 2000 Professional forms the client component of a network environment for groups of business users, working in collaboration with other members of the Windows 2000 family which provide the server and systems management functions.

Windows 2000 Server

Windows 2000 Professional continues as the operating system for the desktop and mobile client machines that connect to the network and access the servers.

For increased reliability, the server PC should be dedicated to that task. This provides the opportunity to add further server functions to the system. The Server part of the Windows 2000 family consists of three versions (each contains the functionality of the Professional edition), with additional capabilities meeting different business needs. The Windows 2000 Server supports servers and administrators on multipurpose networks for workgroups and small business environments, adding the security

and management capabilities that Windows 2000 Professional alone cannot support.

Windows 2000 Advanced Server

This is designed for e-commerce and larger business applications. It includes everything that is in Windows 2000 Server plus improvements in availability and scalability features to support higher volumes of users and more complex applications.

In Advanced Server, 2-node Cluster service supports fail-over – caused by hardware or software failure – of critical applications, including databases, knowledge management, ERP, and file and print services. The 32-node Network Load Balancing (NLB) enables you to develop your network or Internet site by simply adding machines. NLB then directs traffic on the site to spread it across the multiple machines. This technology also makes it possible to take servers off-line for repair or upgrade without interrupting the service to users.

Windows 2000 Datacenter Server

This completes the family. It includes all the Advanced Server features plus greater processing and memory capabilities to meet the needs of intensive on-line transaction processing (OLTP), large data warehouses and large Internet and Application service providers (ISPs and ASPs).

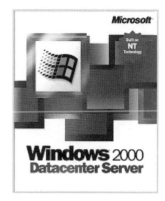

Datacenter Server also provides cascading fail-over among four nodes, and will support 32-node Network Load Balancing for performance and reliability.

Functions offered by Advanced Server and Datacenter Server are far beyond the requirements of small businesses, but they demonstrate the growth path that the Windows 2000 family can offer.

Windows 2000 Professional

This is the edition of Windows 2000 for the desktop and mobile client PC, and the replacement for Windows NT 4 Workstation or Windows 98.

Windows 2000 Professional combines the ease of using Windows 98 with the manageability, reliability and security of Windows NT. This makes it the operating system of choice for use on the Internet, in the office, at home or on a mobile or notebook PC.

Windows 2000 Professional uses the Windows interface familiar from Windows 98, with some enhancements:

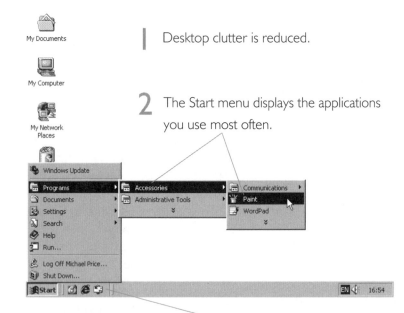

1 Desktop clutter is reduced.

2 The Start menu displays the applications you use most often.

See page 30 for details of the Start menu and page 118 for personalised program menus.

3 The Taskbar includes the Quick Launch bar – it can be customised and repositioned and can have toolbars added to it.

There are step-by-step wizards provided for many tasks such as adding hardware or selecting printers.

4 The Add Network Place wizard helps you locate and add links to shared folders or Web pages, giving you examples of address formats and providing a Browse button to search for nearby PCs.

Windows 2000 allows you to sample multimedia file content without actually opening the file.

Windows 2000 makes the system easy to use in small ways too. It displays file information and provides previews for multimedia files, sound, image and video.

5 Select any file to see its name, type and size.

6 If it's an audio or video file, click Play to sample it.

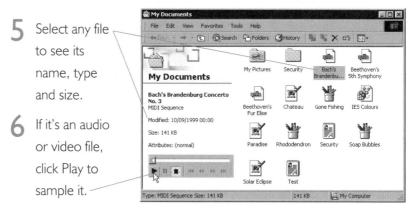

7 If you select a graphics file, a thumbnail image of the contents will be shown.

It's not just easier to use, it's quicker too. Windows 2000 can achieve performance levels that would not be feasible in Windows 98, even with extra memory, and it provides tools to check and optimise the performance of your system.

8 You can change the View in specific folders to display all graphics files as thumbnails instead of icons.

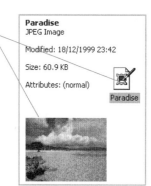

Windows 2000 Professional is faster than Windows NT Workstation or Windows 98. With 64 megabytes of memory, it performs on average 25 percent faster than Windows 98, and you can run more programs and perform more tasks at the same time because of the 32-bit architecture. Each application runs in its own memory space. This means that, when one application fails, it doesn't bring down the whole system.

Adding more memory to the PC makes the improvement even greater, and the scope for expansion is enormous. It supports up to four gigabytes of memory and, if your PC hardware permits the installation of a second processor, you can double the processing power and take advantage of two-way symmetric multiprocessing.

Windows 2000 licences

If you have an existing PC running Windows 98, you will be able to upgrade to Windows 2000 Professional, but not to any Server edition.
The same rule applies to NT 3.51/4.0 workstation.

The main types of licence offered for Windows 2000 are:

- Standard (for a PC without qualifying software).

- Version Upgrade (for a PC with NT installed).

- Competitive Upgrade (for a PC with qualifying competitive software).

The qualifying software includes Novell, Banyan, IBM, LANtastic and other networking systems, Sun systems and various Unix systems, as well as various Microsoft networking and operating system software.

The upgrade paths supported are:

Upgrade from	Upgrade to Profess.	Server	Advanced	DC
Win CE (all versions)	-	-	-	-
Win 3.x	-	-	-	-
Win 95/98/98 SE	X	-	-	-
Win NT 3.51 Workstation	X	-	-	-
Win NT 4.0 Workstation	X	-	-	-
Win 2000 Professional **	X	-	-	-
Win NT 3.51 Server	-	X	X*	-
Win NT 4.0 Server	-	X	X*	-
Win NT 4.0 Term Server	-	X	X*	-
Win NT 4.0 Enterprise Ed	-	-	X	X
BackOffice SBE 4.x	-	-	-	-
NT 4.0 Embedded	-	-	-	-
Win 2000 Server **	-	X	-	-
Win 2000 Adv Server **	-	-	X	X
Win 2000 DC Server	-	-	-	X
Competitive upgrade	X	X	X	X

*   To Advanced server full version only.
**   Beta 3 or later.

This Web page also helps you check the requirements, and there is a link to the hardware and software (and BIOS) compatibility site.

As the table illustrates, the upgrade paths offered are quite complex so check the latest situation at the Microsoft website for Windows 2000 Professional information and resources.

Connect to the Web and visit `http://www.microsoft.com/windows2000/professional/default.asp`.

Requirements

The minimum hardware requirements for Windows 2000 Professional are:

Before you install Windows 2000 Professional, make sure your PC meets the requirements.

- One or two 133 MHz Pentium or equivalent processors.

- 32 MB memory (64 MB is recommended, and 4 GB is the maximum).

- 2 GB hard disk with a minimum of 650 MB disk space free.

The minimum specification is what is needed to install Windows 2000. There is no allowance for applications or data, so you must allow more disk space and memory.

- Monitor and adapter support for 640 x 480 VGA or higher resolution (800 x 600 256-colour recommended).

- Keyboard.

- Mouse or compatible pointing device (optional).

For installation from CD-ROM:

- A CD-ROM or DVD drive (12x or faster recommended).

- A high-density 3.5 inch disk drive (unless your PC system BIOS supports booting from the CD-ROM).

For installation over the network:

- Windows 2000-compatible network adapter card and appropriate cable and hub connection.

- Access to the shared network drive that contains the Windows 2000 Setup files.

Windows 2000 Setup automatically checks your hardware and software and reports any potential conflicts. To check out your PC or devices before running setup, view the Hardware Compatibility List (file HCL.TXT) in the Support folder on the installation CD. Check also that you have Windows 2000 device drivers and that you have the latest system BIOS for your PC.

Methods of installing

Most PCs arrive with the needed operating system already installed.

The way in which you install Windows 2000 depends on the type of system currently installed on your PC. There are three main methods you could use:

- New installation/complete replacement.

- Upgrade from current operating system.

- Update, retaining current operating system.

The first option is used when you want to start from scratch with a new or reformatted disk drive. You must provide the information required for regional settings and network settings and any other configuration information that the setup program cannot obtain automatically. Install your applications and utilities to complete the setup.

Don't upgrade the system if there are any existing device or configuration errors.

If you have a working system that is compatible, for example Windows 95/98 or NT 4.0, you can upgrade to Windows 2000 and retain the existing configuration settings for applications, devices and network connections. This is the quickest and easiest method and involves the minimum interaction, since the information needed for upgrading is taken from your current installation.

This is the option to choose when you want to learn about the new system.

If you want to install Windows 2000, but you are not yet ready to give up your existing system, you can add the new system but keep the current system in operation. This is known as dual-boot, since you have a choice of two systems at start-up. Setup will require more interaction, since you'll need to select the Windows 2000 configuration options. When installation is completed, you must also install a second copy of each application or utility that you want to use with Windows 2000.

Sharing a partition between operating systems may appear to work, but causes unexpected errors and conflicts.

If you choose the dual-boot approach, you should install the Windows 2000 system in a separate hard disk or partition. The Setup program does give you the option to install Windows 2000 in the same partition, and this may appear to work, since the system files and folders are in Winnt rather than Windows, keeping registry files, desktops etc. separate. However, when you add applications, there will still be conflicts, since both operating systems will be installing applications to the Program Files folder.

New installation

To install Windows 2000 onto a new or reformatted hard disk, you must start up the PC using the set of four Setup diskettes provided.

You can use your Windows 98 start-up diskette if you want to format the partition to remove existing software.
Run Setup.exe from the Windows 2000 CD-ROM to start the installation.

1 Boot the PC from the first Setup diskette. This immediately runs Setup.exe, which checks the PC configuration and then starts operating, initially in MS-DOS text mode.

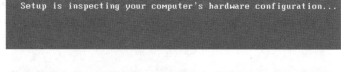

    Setup is inspecting your computer's hardware configuration...

    Windows 2000 Setup

You may be able to start setup directly from the CD-ROM to install Windows 2000 without needing diskettes (see page 20).

2 Insert Setup disks 2, 3 and 4 in turn, as prompted and Setup copies all the files needed to start Windows 2000, storing the files on a RAMdisk in memory.

    Windows 2000 Professional Setup

    Welcome to Setup.
    This portion of the Setup program prepares Microsoft(R)
    Windows 2000(TM) to run on your computer.

    • To set up Windows 2000 now, press ENTER.
    • To repair a Windows 2000 installation, press R.
    • To quit Setup without installing Windows 2000, press F3.

If you have already installed Windows 2000 but need to repair the system, select R.

3 Press F3 if you change your mind, or press Enter to continue to set up a new installation of Windows 2000.

The setup process

You may be requested to enter a CD key, unless you are installing from a network drive.

1 Press F8 to confirm that you agree to the Microsoft terms and conditions. There's no room for negotiation – your only other option is to use another OS such as LINUX instead.

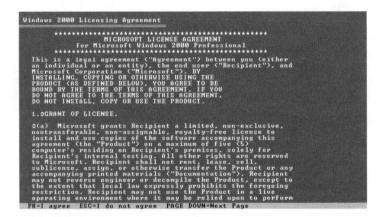

2 Setup will show the hard disks on your PC, with the partitions already defined and/or the free space available.

There are a number of options for formatting and partitioning the hard disk, and for installing Windows 2000 on a second hard disk. Windows 2000 provides administrative tools for managing your hard disk.

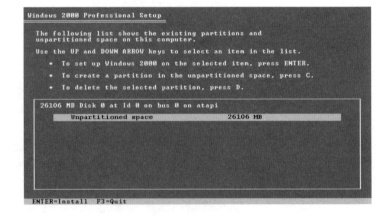

You could use the NTFS file system, but for home or small office use, the FAT system may be faster and more suitable.

3 Press C to create a partition in an area of free space. If it is larger than 2048 MB, setup uses the FAT32 file system rather than FAT16. Setup formats the partition, copies the files required to install and configure Windows 2000, then restarts the PC.

GUI setup

When the system restarts, Setup continues in graphical rather than text mode, as the logo screen demonstrates.

GUI stands for Graphical User Interface.

At this point, you'll see no less than three different displays, all asking you to wait while Windows 2000 starts up.

| | The Setup wizard starts and analyses your system. This may take 15 minutes or so, depending on the configuration of your PC. |

2 Click Locale Customise, and select English, United Kingdom, to configure how numbers, dates and currencies are displayed.

3 Click Keyboard Customise to change the keyboard layout definition, and select the English, United Kingdom layout.

You can select two or more keyboard layouts, and specify hot keys to switch between them.

4 Enter your name and (optionally) your organisation. These details will be used later when you install applications.

Setup continues until it reaches the stage where it requires names for the PC, the user account and the network.

Administration

1 Specify a name for the PC. If you are connected to a network, check with the administrator for the name to use.

Setup will suggest a randomly generated name. This is unlikely to be useful and is best replaced by a name that represents the role, location or purpose of the PC.

Windows 2000 Professional Setup

Computer Name and Administrator Password
You must provide a name and an Administrator password for your computer.

Setup has suggested a name for your computer. If your computer is on a network, your network administrator can tell you what name to use.

Computer name: DELL

Setup creates a user account called Administrator. You use this account when you need full access to your computer.

Type an Administrator password.

Administrator password: **********

Confirm password: **********

< Back   Next >

Don't enter a null password or an obvious value, since that could leave you vulnerable to attack from users on the Internet.

2 Setup creates an administrator account, from which the system can be controlled and managed. Provide a secure password.

You should also create a standard user account for your normal day-to-day use of the PC, and reserve the Administrator account for making system changes such as adding new users.

Setup does not choose the time zone for you, even though you've specified the locale.

3 Check the date and time specified for your PC, and select the time zone that applies to your location.

With dual-boot or multiple systems on your PC, only one should be enabled for summer time.

4 If this is the main or only operating system on the PC, select to automatically adjust for summer time.

5 Setup installs the networking components based on the communications devices that it has detected on your PC.

Setup from CD

Start up this way if you have a non-bootable partition on the hard disk or if you delete the existing partition.

The system BIOS on the modern PC will support booting from CD-ROM. To start setup on a PC with an empty, unformatted hard disk:

1 Insert the CD into the CD drive, make sure there is no diskette inserted and then switch on the PC.

If the BIOS on your PC does not support booting from CD-ROM, you must use setup diskettes. If these are not supplied, use Makedisk from the setup CD to create a set.

2 The BIOS loads and checks for a bootable partition on the hard disk. Finding none, it checks the CD-ROM and loads its boot image, which in its turn starts Windows 2000 Setup.

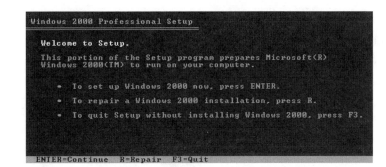

3 Setup proceeds just as described for installation starting from diskette, except that there is no need to insert or remove diskettes.

To boot from CD on a PC with an existing bootable partition, run the BIOS setup utility to change the boot sequence:

You should set Removable Devices, CD-ROM, Hard Drive and then Network Boot. Restore the original sequence when you've finished Setup, to avoid problems with other bootable CDs.

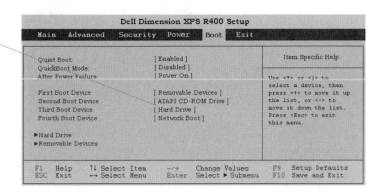

Upgrading your PC

If you have Windows 98 or Windows NT 4 on your PC, you do not need to boot from diskette or CD, and the configuration can be simpler, since Setup will take advantage of the current configuration to specify the new settings.

Windows 2000 needs more resources than Windows 98, so check that your PC matches memory and processor requirements.

| Select Device Manager in System Properties and check that all devices are working correctly. Also check that there are no "unknown device" entries.

2 Close all applications and insert the Windows 2000 CD.

If AutoRun has been disabled, run Setup.exe from the CD to start the upgrade.

3 AutoRun starts the Setup program which detects that there is an older version of Windows currently installed.

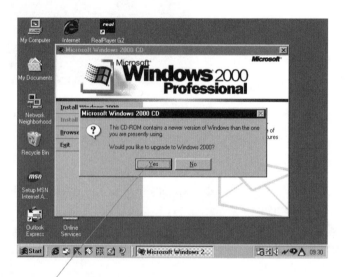

4 Select Yes to begin the upgrade to Windows 2000.

Before the upgrade starts, Setup will request any application upgrade files you may have.

5 Select Upgrade to Windows 2000 to replace the current system (while taking advantage of the existing settings).

The report may tell you of items that must be removed before you carry out the upgrade, so it is worth examining it in detail. If you save a copy, it will be found in the root as Upgrade.txt.

6 Setup prepares a report on your hardware and software, which you can view and save or print.

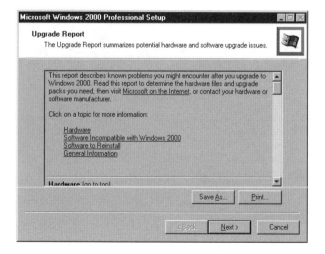

7 Press Next and Setup upgrades the system, without any interaction.

The upgraded system

When the upgrade completes, you'll find your original desktop customised for Windows 2000.

Among the changes is a new choice of background colours from teal to medium blue. You'll also see My Network Places, not Network Neighbourhood, but it does retain the device sharing.

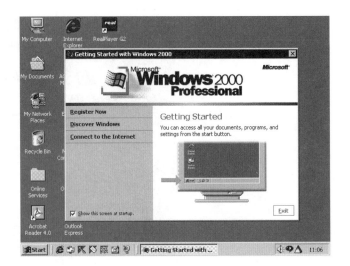

2 When you display the Start menu, you'll see all your old, familiar entries, plus some new Windows 2000 entries.

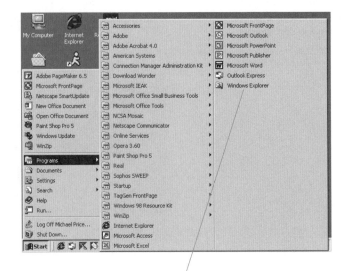

You can change the desktop layout to make it more like the original if you wish (see page 106).

3 Entries are now sorted and overflow to a second panel.

Retaining the old system

If you are not sure of Windows 2000 and just want to try it out, install it without losing or changing your current system.

1 Start the Setup program as before, but this time opt to install a new copy of Windows 2000.

2 You'll now be asked to provide details such as locale and keyboard, since no use is made of the existing settings.

Unless you change the file copy options, the new system will install into the same partition as the existing system. This is not recommended.

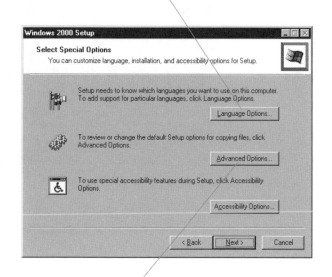

3 Select the Advanced Options to change settings for copying files.

...cont'd

You can partition your hard drive to create extra primary or logical drives. A separate utility such as PartitionMagic makes this easier.

The Setup will run just like a new installation except that the old system remains on the disk, and you can access either system from the startup boot menu.

4 Opt to choose the drive or partition to install Windows 2000. Setup will then offer this option during the upgrade.

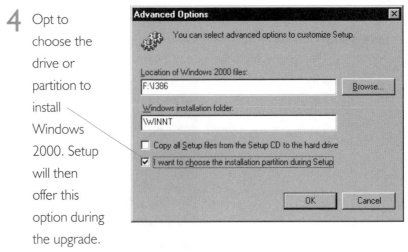

5 The system restarts and runs Setup as a new installation. It stops (if you set the option) for you to pick the partition.

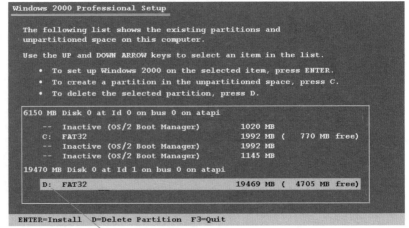

6 Choose the partition or free space area which will contain the new system. Here, for example, you'd choose the D: drive on the second hard disk.

Setup will format the partition if required, copy the files needed and restart the system to install Windows 2000.

Exploring Windows 2000

This chapter explores the Windows 2000 Desktop and the components that appear when you start the system. It also looks at the contents of My Computer and the options for files and folders and other features of the Desktop.

Covers

Initial tasks | 26

Desktop items | 27

My Computer folders | 28

Start menu | 30

Search assistance | 31

Recent Documents | 32

Program groups | 33

Starting programs | 34

Additional components | 36

Taskbar and toolbars | 37

Closing down | 38

Explorer view | 39

Files and folders | 40

Context menu | 42

Send To | 43

Registered file types | 44

Chapter Two

Initial tasks

When Windows starts for the first time, it presents the Getting Started with Windows 2000 screen, with the following actions:

You don't have to perform all these tasks immediately. Click the box to prevent the display showing each time Windows starts up:

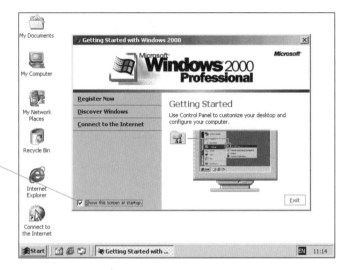

I Register Now – this registers your copy of Windows 2000. It sends your details to Microsoft, via the modem and telephone line, and makes you eligible for Windows Update.

It is not essential to send details of your hardware and software with your registration, since Windows Update will analyse your PC locally (see pages 185–186).

If you have switched off the Getting Started with Windows 2000 screen, select it from the Systems Tools list in the Start menu to run the tour.

2 Discover Windows – this runs the Discover 2000 tour, which introduces various categories of information about the system. You'll need the Windows installation CD.

3 Connect to the Internet – this helps you to specify your Internet Service Provider (ISP) and account details, or to connect to an ISP to obtain a new account.

Desktop items

Folders left open when you shut down will be reopened when you restart. Programs will not be restarted.

The specific layout of your Windows 2000 Desktop will depend on the options installed on your system; the changes that you make to customise the machine; and the contents of the Desktop at the time it was last shut down. Typically however, you will find these components:

My Documents – the folder for your work-in-progress or completed work

My Computer – the drives and devices in your PC

My Network Places – PCs and other devices available via the LAN

Recycle Bin – intermediate storage for deleted files

Internet Explorer – access points for the World Wide Web

Start Button – access to the Start menu of application groups, programs and tools

Quick Launch bar and Taskbar – clear Desktop, select applications or folders and store toolbars

System Tray – quick access to system tools and utilities

My Computer folders

The folder shows all the drives, fixed or removable. The other devices on your PC can be found in the Control Panel folder.

1 Double-click the My Computer icon on the Desktop.

My Computer

You can also open My Computer in Explorer view. See page 39 for details.

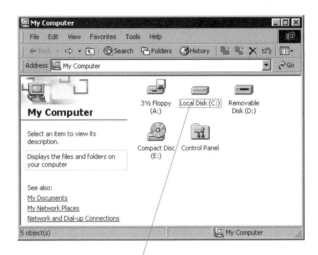

2 Double-click one of the drive icons to see all the files and folders contained in its root folder.

If you change folder options to display separate windows by default, the action of the Ctrl key is reversed.

3 Double-click a folder to view its contents. By default, each new window appears in place of the previous window. Hold down Ctrl as you open the folder to display its contents in a separate window.

For important folders such as Winnt and Program Files, the contents may not be displayed automatically.

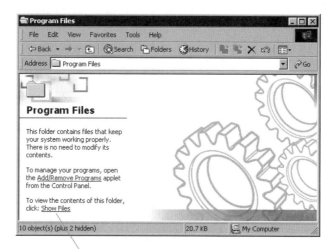

4 Click the Show Files link to display the details of the folder contents.

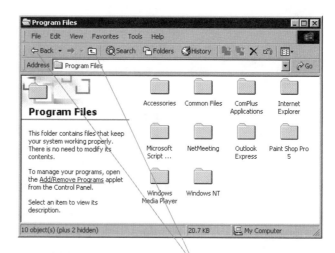

There is a link to the Control Panel also. See page 46 for the contents of this folder.

5 Click the forward and backward arrows to navigate through your selections, or click the Up arrow button to navigate through the drive folder structure.

Start menu

To display the contents of the Start menu, press the Start button on the Taskbar. The shortcut entries and folders on the Start menu depend on the applications installed and on the settings chosen, but you should find most of these menu entries:

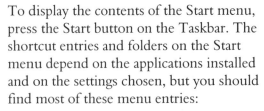

- Access the **Windows Update** site on the Internet to upgrade the system.

- The **Programs** entry displays lists of applications and menus. You can drag-and-drop entries to customise these menus.

- **Favorites** allows you to open websites that you have previously visited and book-marked. This list is also on the menu bars in My Computer, My Network Places, Windows Explorer, Control Panel, and even the Recycle Bin.

- **Settings** has commands to display the Control Panel, Networking and Printers options, as well as adjusting the Start menu settings.

- **Search** will look for files or folders on your drives, for documents and websites on the Internet, or for People via directory services and address books.

- Other entries include **Help** to display information and troubleshooting aids, and the **Run** command to locate and execute application programs.

- Select **Log off** to end your session and allow another user to Log on to Windows 2000.

Search assistance

If your keyboard has the Win key, press Win+F to start the Search.

The Search command, previously known as Find, assists you when you know that a document is somewhere on the hard disk, but you just can't remember where you saved it. It supports simple searches by file name or more advanced searches using whatever information you have: date, file type, keywords, etc. To start the Search command:

1   Press Start, Search, Files or Folders to open Windows Explorer with the Search bar ready to use.

If there are several drives on your PC, you can search all local hard disks with the one Search. Select Look In, Local Harddrives (C:).

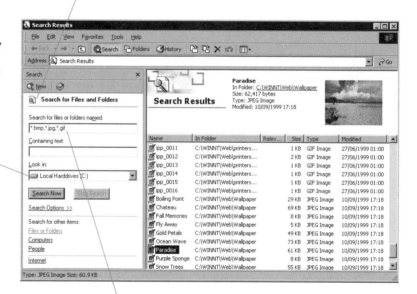

If you get a long list, you can refine the search to help locate the required file, for example by adding a key word or phrase from the document to the Containing text box.

2   Type the file name. You can enter just part of the name, or use wild cards (e.g. *.bmp), and put multiple values.

3   Select the drive or browse to the folder that should contain the file, and press Search Now.

4   You'll get a list of all the files that match. The file details, and a thumbnail for images, are shown for the highlighted file.

Recent Documents

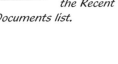

Not all applications are able to add their files to the Recent Documents list.

If you are trying to locate a document that you have recently been working with, don't overlook the Recent Documents list which keeps track of the last twenty or so data or program files that you have worked with. To open a file from the list:

1 Click Start and then select Documents. You'll see a list of your recent documents, multimedia and data files.

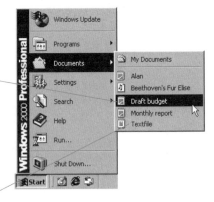

If all else fails, look in the Recycle Bin where you may be able to find and restore a deleted copy of the file.

2 Click the name of the document you want to open, and the associated application starts up with that document loaded.

Clearing the history

1 Click Start, Settings, Taskbar & Start Menu and click the Advanced tab.

You can also right-click a clear part of the Taskbar and select Properties to display the panel.

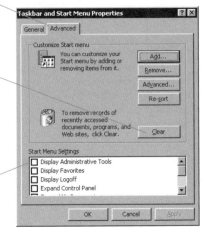

2 Click the Clear button to clear the records in the document list. This does not delete the files themselves.

3 The Settings section is also used to restyle the Start menu.

Program groups

You can find out what is installed by looking in Start, Programs, Accessories and its subfolders.

There are many application programs, tools and utilities provided with Windows 2000. Most of these will already be installed on your PC and included in your Start menu folders. They are selected by default during Setup, unless your administrator has modified the standard selection.

The groups of programs include:

1   Tools to allow you to access the Internet, send email and maintain your Windows 2000 system.

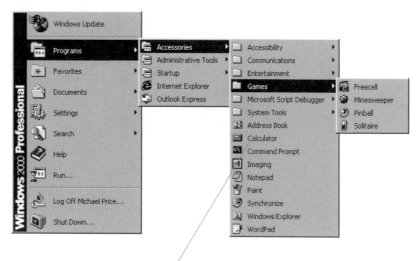

2   Accessories such as Calculator, Windows Explorer and WordPad that provide a basic set of office functions, not to mention a set of games – for mouse practice, perhaps.

You will also find tools for Multimedia, Fax, Systems, Administration and Communications.

3   Accessibility options that make the PC display and keyboard easier to manage. These are intended for users with impaired hearing or restricted vision. However, the functions can offer very useful support to any Windows 2000 user.

Starting programs

If the program you want is not in the Start menu, click Start, Search, Files or Folders, and use the Search Assistant to locate the program file.

To start a program, locate the appropriate entry in the Start menu and click to run. For example, to start Calculator and WordPad:

1 Click Start, Programs, Accessories and Calculator to launch the Calculator program.

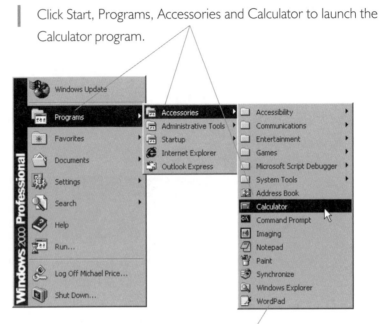

2 Click Start, Programs, Accessories, WordPad to start that program.

The names of the active programs are displayed along the Taskbar.

The names of any open folders will also appear in the Taskbar, and you can switch between folders, or minimise and restore folder windows also.

3 Click the program name on the Taskbar to make its window active. Click another name to switch programs.

4 Click the active name on the Taskbar to minimise its window and select the next program. Click the minimised program to redisplay its window and make it the active program.

5 You can also press Ctrl+Tab to list the open programs and switch active windows.

When you've finished working with an application, there are several ways to stop running the associated program:

Some programs, such as Calculator, do not have a menu sequence for quitting, so you must use the Title bar methods.

1 Double-click the control icon on the left of the Title bar or click the Close button on the right of the Title bar.

2 Press Alt+F4, or select the quit sequence (e.g. File, Close) from the active application. The exact form will depend on the particular program.

3 Right-click the name on the Taskbar and select Close from the menu.

In each of these cases, you will be prompted to save any open data files if you have made any changes to their content.

Additional components

There are some extra Windows components on the Windows 2000 installation CD. To install these:

This shows the Start menu with the option, Use Personalised Menus (see page 118) unset, so all Control Panel entries are displayed.

1 Click Start, Settings, Control Panel, Add/Remove Programs.

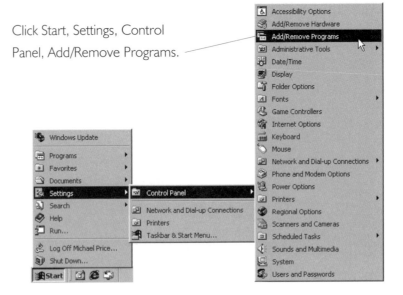

2 Click Add/Remove Windows Components. Select a box to add an item, or clear it to remove an already installed item.

The Indexing Service, and other tools are provided as Windows components. You'll also find tools and documentation in the Resource Kit on the Install CD.

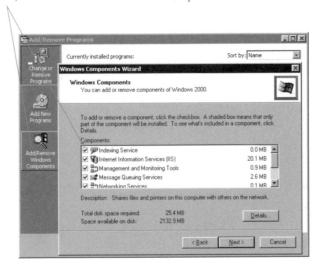

3 Click Next to copy, configure and install the components.

Taskbar and toolbars

As well as the Start button and the entries for active programs and open windows, the Taskbar contains the Quick Launch bar and the System Tray.

The Quick Launch bar is intended for shortcuts to any programs that you use often, but Internet programs are the default entries:

Internet Explorer, the
Internet browser

Outlook Express, the
email program

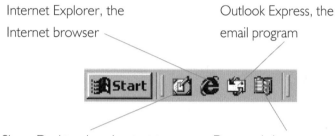

This is an alternative to the Win+M and Win+Shift+M keystrokes, or the Win+D toggle option.

Show Desktop is a shortcut to clear the Desktop. It minimises (and next time maximises) all open and active windows

Drag-and-drop a program icon from Windows Explorer onto the Quick Launch bar to add a new entry

The System Tray has icons for resident tools and utilities, usually installed at start-up time. The entries depend on the hardware installed, but typical entries include:

Add other toolbars onto the Taskbar, including the Address bar, the Links bar and the Desktop bar (the Desktop icons in a toolbar), or create your own toolbar (see page 122).

Input Locale (language) selector

The CD-RW device

The print spooler (appears when printing is active)

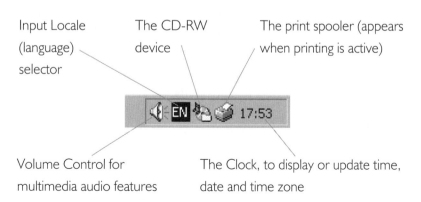

Volume Control for multimedia audio features

The Clock, to display or update time, date and time zone

Closing down

One more thing to do, before continuing the exploration of Windows 2000, is to make sure that you know how to stop. Closing down the PC properly is an essential part of using the system effectively.

Alt+F4 is a universal Close that ends the current window or application. Pressing this several times will bring you to the Shutdown window.

1 Close all open windows and end all active programs.

2 Select Start, Shut down and choose the shutdown type.

Any file folders left open will be remembered and reopened next time you use the system.

3 Click OK to action the shut down, or Cancel to return to Windows.

You can choose to Restart, Logoff or Shutdown.

Restart — if you want to refresh the system, for example if unexpected problems arise after you have been running for a long period. There may be problems with Windows resources, especially if you start and stop applications a number of times.

Logoff — if you plan to relinquish the PC so that another user can sign on to it. This will protect your personal settings and your document and image folders.

Other Shutdown options may appear, if there is support on your PC for the advanced power management options.

Shut down — if you have finished working with your system and you are ready to switch it off. Windows will write all unsaved data to the hard disk and prepare the machine for power-off. It may even activate power-off for you.

You may have **Stand by**, **Hibernate** or **Disconnect** options, depending on the level of power management support on the PC.

Explorer view

You can also open Windows Explorer from the Start menu, by selecting Start, Programs, Accessories, Windows Explorer.

Double-clicking My Computer launches the default Folder view (without the Folder bar).
To view the Folder bar, follow step 2.

By default, the drives and folders are shown in folder view (see page 28) but you can switch to the Windows Explorer view.

Whichever view you start in, click the Folders button to toggle the view.

You can use Windows Explorer to view the contents of My Computer, to access files and folders contained on your drives, including the floppy disk, the hard disk, removable drives such as Iomega Zip disks, the CD-ROM drive and any network drives.

1   To open My Computer directly in Windows Explorer view, right-click the icon and choose Explore.

2   If My Computer is already open, select View, Explorer Bar, Folders, or click the Folders button on the toolbar, to toggle between Folder and Explorer view.

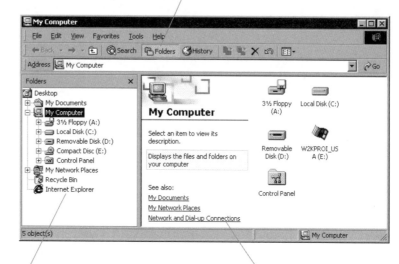

Folder
bar

3   Click the links to switch between My Computer, My Documents, My Network Places or Network and Dial-up Connections. You'll find return links in the new view, or you can click the Back button.

Files and folders

The My Computer folder has the following options: Large Icons, Small Icons, List and Details.
File folders have one additional option: Thumbnails.

The default folder view shows large icons, but you can change the types of icons and the level of detail that is displayed in a folder.

To change the view characteristics:

1 Select View from the Menu bar and choose a folder display.

2 Choose Details to see the name, size, type and dates when the items were last modified.

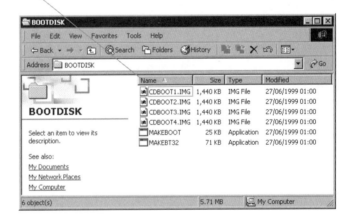

There's also an option to disable the Web view for folders, whatever size of window you choose.

3 If you gradually reduce the size of the window, at some point Explorer automatically drops the Web style information, to leave more space for the folder entries.

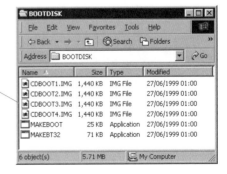

...cont'd

You can select a range of icons using the Shift key, or hold down Ctrl and select the individual icons.

4 To move or copy files and folders, select the icons for the items required and click the Move to or Copy to buttons.

The folder you choose will be remembered and offered as the default choice for the next move or copy.

5 Navigate to the target folder and click OK to move or copy the selection.

6 You will be warned if the new item will overwrite an existing item with the same name.

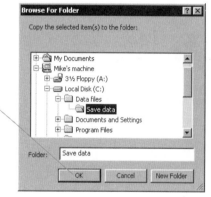

There are no Cut and Paste buttons on the default toolbar, but you can add these when you customise the toolbar.

7 For the usual cut/copy and paste operations via the clipboard, you should select the icons and click Edit on the Menu bar.

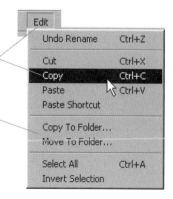

The Edit menu also has entries for the Move to Folder and Copy to Folder options and it provides assistance with selecting items via Select All and Invert Selection. You can also use the Shift or Ctrl keys to select multiple items.

Context menu

Highlight the icon or group of icons and right-click the selection to display the context menu.

The functions listed depend on the file type and on the applications that have been installed on your PC. Typically, you will see the following:

- **Open** – executes the selection using the registered application.

- **Print** – prints the selection (for documents and images).

- **Open With** – opens with an alternative program.

- **Send To** – see page 43.

- **Cut** or **Copy** – self-explanatory.

- **Delete** – self-explanatory.

- **Rename** – self-explanatory.

- **Properties** – displays Properties.

2 For a folder, you are offered Open, Explore or Search.

3 There are Open (without starting), Play, Record and Open With for audio files.

4 For multiple document applications such as Internet Explorer, you'll see Open, Open in Same Window, Print or Open With.

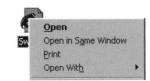

Send To

With the Send To option, you can easily transfer a file to another disk, PC or person.

Sending a file or folder to a disk sends a copy, leaving the original file or folder in place.

To select a destination and send one or more files:

Locate the folder containing the files and select the files that you want to transfer.

Pie Charts   Equipment

Open
Print
Open With...

Send To ▶
        3½ Floppy (A)
Cut   Desktop (create shortcut)
Copy   Mail Recipient
Create Shortcut My Documents
Delete   Removable Disk (D)
Rename

Properties

2 Insert the target disk (if removable) and right-click the selected files.

3 Select Send To and then pick the destination.

The target may be a floppy disk, the Desktop (as a shortcut), an email message, the My Documents folder or a removable drive (if one is installed). There could be other pre-defined destinations, depending on your PC configuration and software setup.

If you send a file to a destination that already has a copy, you can choose to replace it or skip the copy.

When you install devices such as infrared links, these may be added to the list of destinations. You can add other destinations, such as a fax or a folder, to the Send To list, by adding shortcuts to the Send To folder, which is in the Windows folder.

Each user name in Windows 2000 has a separate personal Send To folder, so each user can define a specific set of destinations for sending files and folders and can modify that set without affecting other users.

The Send To folders are hidden by default. If they are not visible, change the Folder Options to show hidden files and folders.

Registered file types

The data file types used by an application are registered at the time of installation, so Windows 2000 knows how to open them.

1 Open My Computer, select Tools from the Menu bar and then click Folder Options.

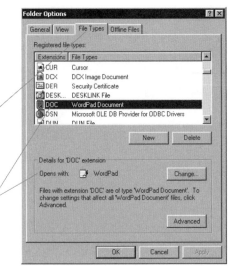

2 Select the File Types tab to see the list of registered file types.

3 Select a file extension to see the associated program.

Select Open With to choose alternative programs for file types that are already registered. Don't select the Always Use... box unless you want to replace the existing default application.

You can add further file types to the list, from Folder Options or when you first open a new type of file.

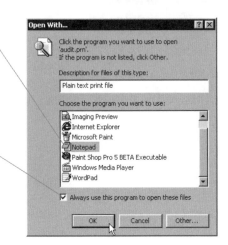

4 Right-click the file icon and select Open from the context menu.

5 Choose a program from the list presented, or click Other... to search for the required application.

6 Select the Always Use... box to make the chosen application the default (i.e. it runs when you double-click the icon).

Windows Components

This chapter looks at Control Panel tools (used to review and adjust the properties of the devices on your PC) and at the applications, utilities and games in the Accessories folder.

Covers

Control Panel options | 46

Add/remove | 48

Date/time | 50

Display | 51

Fonts | 52

Keyboard | 53

Mouse | 54

Start menu accessories | 55

Calculator | 56

Command Prompt | 57

Imaging | 58

Notepad | 59

Paint | 60

WordPad | 61

Entertainment | 62

Games | 64

Windows Explorer | 66

Chapter Three

Control Panel options

The Control Panel allows you to adjust the settings that control the way your PC operates, and add or remove programs and hardware.

To open the Control Panel:

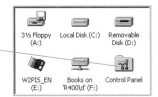

1 Open My Computer and double-click the Control Panel icon.

2 Alternatively, select Start, Settings, Control Panel.

3 In either case, Explorer displays the Control Panel as a folder.

There are 23 icons in this case, but the contents of your Control Panel will differ, depending on the hardware and software that you have installed.

4 Select any icon to view a description. Double-click the icon to open the feature. The following pages examine the main options you can expect to find in your Control Panel.

...cont'd

Accessibility options provide additional functions for users with special needs, but all users could benefit from some of these tools.

The options provided include:

StickyKeys — to input simultaneous keystrokes (e.g. Ctrl+L) while pressing one key at a time.

ToggleKeys — to emit sounds when locking keys are pressed.

SoundSentry and **ShowSounds** — to provide visual cues for sounds and program speech.

High Contrast — to improve screen contrast with alternative colours and font sizes.

MouseKeys — to use the numeric keypad to control the mouse pointer and press the mouse buttons.

To turn on MouseKeys:

If you require higher levels of function, see the Accessibility website at:

`http://www.`
`microsoft.com/`
`isapi/enable/`

1 Open Accessibility Options in the Control Panel and click the Mouse tab.

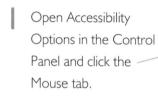

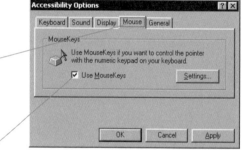

2 Select the Use MouseKeys box, and click Settings.

3 Select Use shortcut to turn MouseKeys on and off by pressing the keys Alt+Shift+Numlock.

MouseKeys are very useful for making precise movements in graphics and drawings.

4 Set the pointer speed and acceleration.

5 Use the Ctrl and Shift keys to speed up or down.

Add/remove

You can add new adapter cards to your PC, connect new devices to connection ports on your PC, or attach devices to USB ports (or PC cards in a laptop PC).

For a new device to work with Windows 2000, a software device driver must be loaded.

To install and activate a new device:

1. Switch off the PC, if required, and insert the adapter. Or connect the device following the manufacturer's instructions.

You can add some devices, USB and PC card devices in particular, without having to switch off or restart your PC.

2. If you need to restart your PC, Windows 2000 should detect the new device and start the Found New Hardware Wizard.

3. If the device is not automatically detected, double-click the Add/Remove Hardware icon in Control Panel and choose Add/Troubleshoot a device.

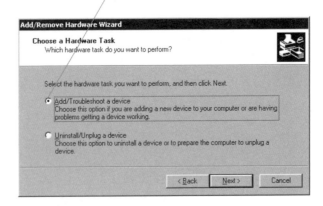

You can install a device without administrator privileges, if an administrator has already loaded the drivers for the device.

4. You must log on as the administrator (or belong to the Administrator group) to run the Add/Remove Hardware Wizard.

To review the list of programs on your PC:

Use Add/ Remove Programs to add a new program, or to change or remove an existing program.

| Open Add/Remove Programs from the Control Panel and click the Change or Remove Programs button.

2 Select a program title and click Change/Remove to revise the configuration or delete an application that was previously added.

Programs that you install are added to the list, which also includes all applications detected when you upgraded from Windows 98 or Windows NT to Windows 2000.

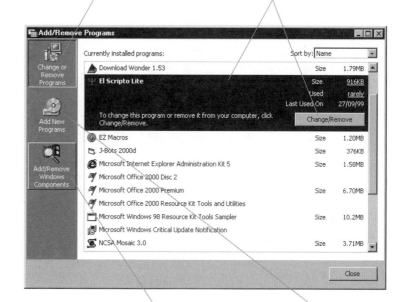

To change Windows components you'll need the administrator level of authority.

3 Click Add/Remove Windows Components to amend the set of additional programs installed from the Windows 2000 CD.

4 Click Add New Programs to add applications from CD or floppy, or to select fixes and new features from Windows Update on the Microsoft website.

If your PC is on a network, you may see a list of additional programs on the Add New Programs screen. This will have been placed on a server by your network administrator for installation over the LAN.

Date/time

1 Open Date/Time in the Control Panel and select the Date & Time tab.

2 Select the month.

Adjust the year setting.

Choose the day number.

Adjust the hours, minutes or seconds.

You can also open Date/Time by double-clicking the time in the System tray. If the time doesn't currently appear:

Click Start, Settings, Taskbar & Start Menu, select Show clock and then double-click the time to show Date & Time properties.

Changing time zones:

1 Select the Time Zone tab, click the down-arrow and select the required time zone.

2 You can have the clock adjust itself automatically for summer time, as defined in that time zone.

Display

You can control how your desktop looks and how your monitor displays information, and completely customise the colours and fonts that are used in Windows.

To specify colour settings or change your screen resolution:

1 Open Display from the Control Panel and select Settings.

2 Change colour or resolution settings.

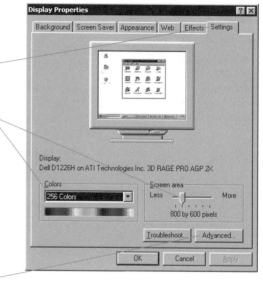

3 To change the refresh rate for your monitor, or to update the display device drivers, click Advanced.

Some of the Display changes require that you be logged on as an administrator.

You can make many changes to the screen and desktop:

Choose a desktop background.

Specify a screen saver to display when your system is idle.

Choose the colours and fonts (if applicable) for the windows elements.

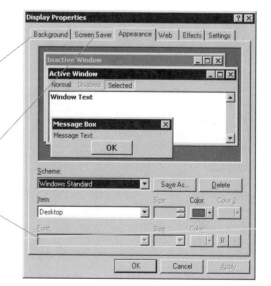

This requires multiple graphics adapters, or the type of graphics adapter that can support two or more monitors.

You can display the windows on separate monitors or spread across two if more than 1 physical display is attached to your PC.

Fonts

Windows 2000 includes a new universal font format, OpenType, which is an extension of the TrueType format used in previous versions of Windows. Both font formats can be scaled and rotated, and displayed in all sizes on any output device.

To view the fonts:

Open the Fonts folder and double-click the Font icon. Double-click a font icon to view font contents and samples.

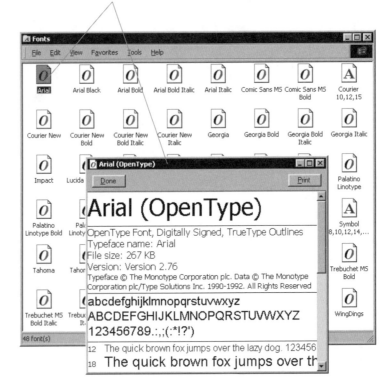

To add a new font:

Copy and paste the font file from the original folder to the Fonts folder.

Arial Alternative Regular

18 Jackdaws love my big sphinx of quartz.

Keyboard

The Keyboard options allow you to make changes to the input locale defined for your PC, and to select new hardware drivers if you change the type of keyboard. It also allows you to change the way your keyboard responds.

For more help with using your keyboard, see the accessibility options and tools (page 47).

1 Open Keyboard in the Control Panel and select the Speed tab.

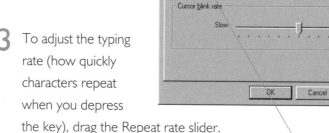

2 To adjust the typing delay (the time before characters repeat) when you depress the key, drag the Repeat delay slider.

3 To adjust the typing rate (how quickly characters repeat when you depress the key), drag the Repeat rate slider.

The Keyboard options allow you to change the rate at which the cursor or insert pointer flashes.

4 Click in the box and hold down a key to check the delay before characters repeat, and the effective rate of repeating.

5 To adjust the cursor blink rate, drag the Cursor blink rate slider.

6 The test cursor to the left of the slider area blinks at the new rate. Click OK or Apply to set the new rates, or click Cancel to drop the changes.

Mouse

The Mouse options allow you to adjust the speed of mouse operation, change the appearance of pointers and add motion effects.

1   Open Mouse in the Control Panel and select the Buttons tab.

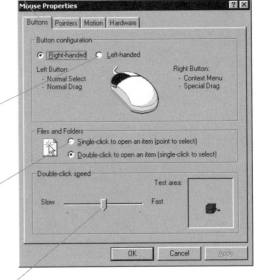

You can also set single-click on or off using the Files and Folders options.

2   To reverse your mouse buttons, select Left-handed.

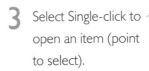

3   Select Single-click to open an item (point to select).

There's a test area for you to try out the double-click setting.

4   To adjust the double-click speed, drag the slider.

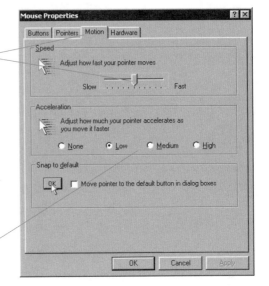

5   Select the Motion tab and drag the Speed slider to change the pointer response.

There's also an option to make the mouse snap to the default button when you switch windows.

6   Specify how quickly the mouse pointer accelerates to its maximum speed.

Start menu accessories

 Some of the applications and utilities are intended for the user, while others (such as the communications and systems programs) are intended for system administrators.

Windows 2000 has a large number of application programs, tools and utilities included. These are not required parts of the operating system as such, but provide the facilities you need to get started using the system, even if you do not initially have any applications or separate programs installed.

Most of these additional programs can be accessed from the Start menu, in the Programs or Accessories menu, or in submenus within those menus.

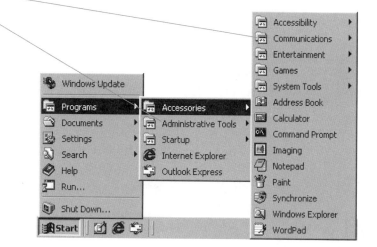

 You'll find fuller function versions or replacements for many of these applications, as separate products from Microsoft or from other software suppliers.

The categories of accessories intended for the user rather than the administrator include:

Accessories:	Calculator, Command Prompt, Imaging, Notepad, Paint, Synchronize, WordPad.
Accessibility:	Magnifier, Narrator, On-Screen Keyboard, Utility Manager, Accessibility Wizard.
Entertainment:	CD Player, Media Player, Sound Recorder, Volume Control.
Games:	Freecell, Minesweeper, Pinball, Solitaire.
Other:	Windows Explorer.

Calculator

You can use your numeric keypad to enter numbers and operators, when Num Lock is on.

The Calculator provides a simple way to carry out calculations on-screen. There are two different views of the Calculator. The standard view is for ordinary calculations:

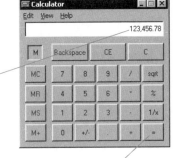

1 Select Start, Programs, Accessories, Calculator.

2 Enter the first number in the calculation and click the operator key (+ - * /).

3 Enter the remaining numbers and operators, and press = to display the result.

The keys include Memory, Backspace, Percentage and Square Root. To check the purpose of any key, right-click it and then click the What's This? button that appears.

You can select the number system (binary, decimal, hexadecimal or octal), use mathematical functions such as sines and logs, or enter statistical data.

For more complex calculations:

4 Click View on the Menu bar and then choose Scientific.

Enter the data using the Sta and Dat keys, and click a statistics function such as Avg or Standard deviation.

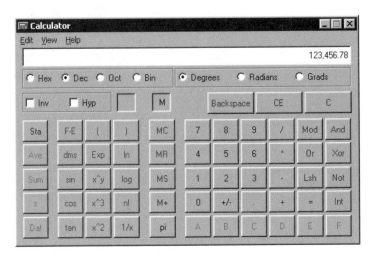

Command Prompt

Although Windows 2000 is not MS-DOS based, it does provide a set of command line functions that extend and enhance what was possible with previous versions of Windows and MS-DOS.

Some of the commands used in MS-DOS are not needed in Windows 2000, others require changes, and there are commands that are new in Windows 2000. To see details of all the commands, view the Windows 2000 Command Reference in the Help file.

To open a Command Prompt:

1. Select Start, Programs, Accessories, Command Prompt. Press Alt+Enter to switch between full screen and window.

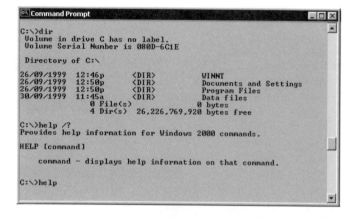

2. Right-click the Title bar of the window, click Properties and select the Layout tab.

A history of up to 50 of the past commands is kept, so you can scroll back and forth through the list.

3. Set screen size and window size, and apply the change to the current or to all command windows.

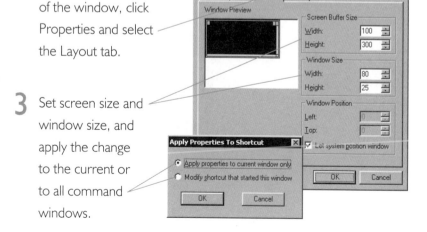

Imaging

Imaging can input .JPG, .PCX, .XIF, .GIF and .WIF images, as well as .TIF, .BMP and .AWD.

Kodak Imaging is designed to work with multipage faxed or scanned documents and with various types of image files, saving documents as .TIF or .BMP images or .AWD faxes. It allows you to view and annotate the documents with text or drawings. There are zoom facilities, and you can rotate the picture through 90 or 180 degree turns. A neat feature is the rubberstamp which allows you to overprint documents with Draft or Date Received etc.

To view an image:

Select Open With, Imaging Preview for quick image load without edit. If Imaging Preview does not appear, click Choose Program to select the required viewer.

1 Locate the image file using Search, My Computer or Windows Explorer.

2 Right-click the document icon and select Open With, Imaging.

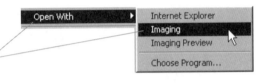

Select Tools, General Options and click the Imaging or Preview button to reset the default viewer for the supported file types.

3 To annotate the document, click the Stamp button, choose the text and click on the image.

Notepad

Notepad handles plain text files up to 64K. For larger files, or to format text, use WordPad instead.

Notepad is a basic text editor that you can use to create simple documents. The most common use for Notepad is to view or edit text (.TXT) files, but it is also used to create source code files such as the HTML for Web pages.

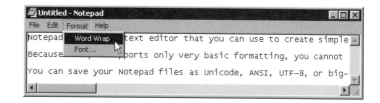

When you open a text file, you may see just one line for each paragraph. To show all the text on the screen:

Wrapping text enables you to see all the text on the line, but it doesn't affect the way text appears when it is printed.

1 Select Format from the Menu bar and click Word Wrap. The entry is ticked to show that Word Wrap is active.

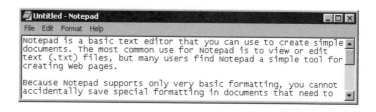

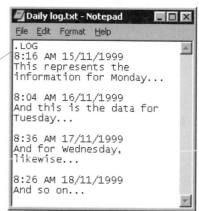

Notepad also has headers and footers, find and replace, and a choice of font (the selected font is applied to the whole document).

To create a log file using Notepad:

2 On the first line of a Notepad document, type the value .LOG at the left margin. Use uppercase and include the stop, then save the document.

Every time you open this document, Notepad will append the current time and date (from the PC clock) to the end of the document.

Paint

Paint can be used for simple drawings and sketches or for highly detailed pictures, since you can control the image pixel by pixel.

Paint works with individual image files in the Windows Bitmap format. With additional graphics filters such as those available in the Office suite, Paint can also read the Internet .GIF and .JPG formats. With this application, you can view or edit a picture, or create your own. There is a range of tools and functions:

1 Select parts of the image, using a rectangle or freehand shape.

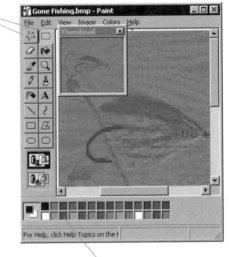

2 Use other tools to erase, fill, colour or magnify selected image parts.

3 Draw with pencil, brush or airbrush tools.

Shapes and text are converted into pixel form so that they can be incorporated into the image.

4 Add text, or lines and shapes to the image.

5 Choose colours from the palette or custom colours.

6 You can zoom the image to make fine changes. The thumbnail image shows the effects at normal size.

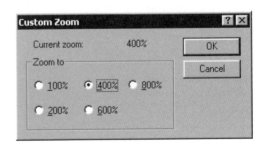

Select the images for wallpaper with care, to avoid making the desktop difficult to read.

There are functions to flip, rotate or skew the image, or the selected part of the image, and to enlarge or reduce the image size by a selected scale factor. You can also convert the bitmap image into a background (wallpaper).

WordPad

WordPad provides word processing functions that are quite suitable for letters and smaller documents. Output is saved in the .RTF format which is compatible with the Microsoft Word formats, though not all Word features are supported.

Drag the bar to an edge to park it horizontally or vertically.

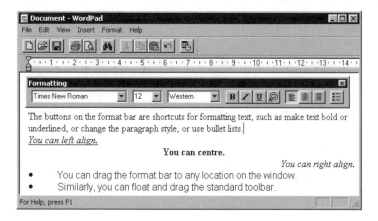

To check the settings for the document:

Select View, Options and choose the tab for the file format you want.

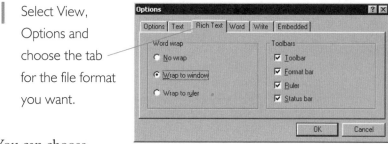

WordPad also supports the Unicode format, which uses two byte coding which provides a universal set of characters for all languages.

You can choose other file formats and specify separate options for each file type. The types supported include Word (.DOC); Write (.WRI), the predecessor to WordPad; the plain text (.TXT) format; and the Embedded Unicode format.

The Word and Write file types incorporate text formatting, but when you save the file as text, any formatting specified will be discarded.

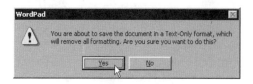

Entertainment

If you have a connection to the Internet, you can download and store the CD details such as artist and track titles.

CD Player

Using CD Player, you can play audio CDs in the background while other tasks are running on your PC. You have full control over the player, so you can play intros, play tracks in any order and pause play. You can create playlists to specify the tracks to play and the order, repeating tracks if you wish.

Microsoft Windows Media Player

File formats supported include: .AVI, .ASF, .ASX, .MID, .MPG, .MPEG, .M1V, .MP2, .MP3, .MPA, .MPE, .RMI, .WAV, .WMA and .WAX.

The Windows Media Player is a universal media player you can use to process audio, video and mixed-media data. You can play files of many different formats, listen to live radio station broadcasts on the Internet, or view video or movie clips on a website.

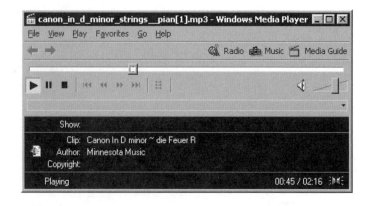

You must be connected to the Internet to check for upgrades.

To get the most recent version of Windows Media Player:

> Select Help, Check for Player Upgrade. If a newer version is available, click Upgrade Now to download.

...cont'd

To record sounds, you must attach a microphone to your sound card.

Recorded sounds are saved as Waveform (.WAV) files.

Click the Speaker icon in the System Tray to display the master volume control. Double-click the icon to display the full Volume Control utility.

Sound Recorder

Using Sound Recorder, you can record, mix, play and edit sounds. You can modify an uncompressed sound file by adding sounds, deleting part of the sound file, changing the playback speed or adding an echo effect. You can even play the sound in reverse.

The sound files can be linked to a document, or inserted as a sound object directly into the document.

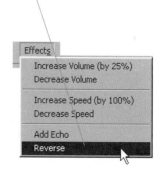

Volume Control

Using Volume Control, you can make adjustments to the input and output sound for the multimedia applications on your PC including CD Player, Media Player, Sound Recorder and other applications such as the DVD Player if installed.

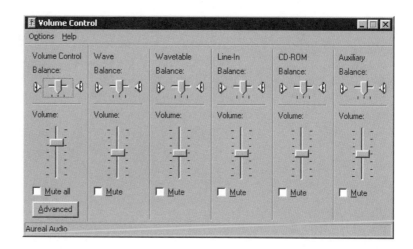

You can change the volume, the balance between the left and right speakers and the bass and treble settings. You may have advanced controls, depending on the type of audio card installed, to make adjustments for surround sound or 3D sound effects.

Games

Every deal can lead to a winning game, so long as you select the right strategy. The key is to keep your free cells unoccupied as much as possible, and to try to make empty columns available.

Freecell

Freecell is a game of Patience. The objective in Freecell is to move all the cards to the home cells, at the top right, using the free cells on the top left as place holders. You build a stack of cards for each suit, starting with the Ace and moving in sequence to the King.

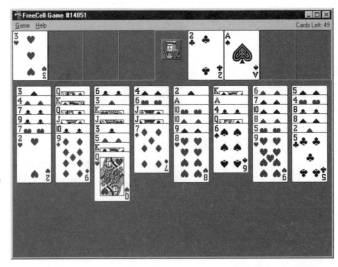

Games are numbered so you can retry a particular game as many times as you wish.

Minesweeper

Minesweeper is a game for one person. The aim is to find all the mines as quickly as possible without uncovering any of them.

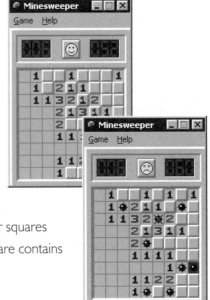

The timer starts when you click the first square.

1 Click Game, New (or press F2) to start a game.

When you succeed at the level designed for beginners, try your skill at one of the higher levels.

2 Uncover a square by clicking it. If it is clear, all adjacent clear squares are also uncovered. If the square contains a mine, you lose the game.

Pinball

The primary goal of the Space Cadet 3D Pinball game is to launch the ball and then earn as many points as possible by hitting bumpers, targets, and flags. The game is divided into nine levels or ranks. The lowest rank is Cadet, and the highest rank is Fleet Admiral. You gain promotion by selecting and completing a series of missions. As you advance, more challenging missions become available.

Regardless of your skill level, you start each game with three balls and the rank of Cadet, and you earn additional balls and rank advancement as you play.

Solitaire

The American version of Patience, Solitaire involves rearranging all the cards in the deck into the four suits, in ascending order starting with the aces.

Make all possible moves on the board before you click the deck to turn over more cards.

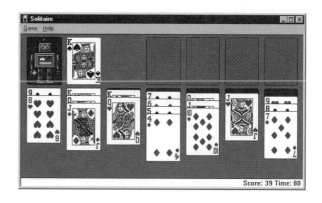

Windows Explorer

To open Windows Explorer from the Start menu:

You can open Windows Explorer from the Start menu, or with Win+E, or with a command in Run or from the Command Prompt.

1 Select Start, Programs, Accessories, Windows Explorer and it starts up in Explore mode with My Documents selected.

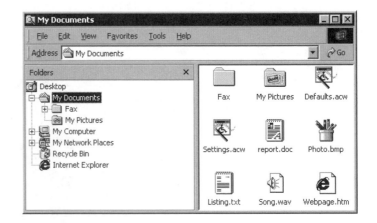

2 Press Win+E, and Windows Explorer starts up in Explore mode with My Computer selected.

3 To start Windows Explorer from the Command Prompt or from Run (and display the folder Win2000 on drive F), you'd enter: explorer.exe /n, /e, /root, f:\win2000

Note that the /e parameter selects Explore mode, while the /root parameter tells Windows Explorer to open the folder as the highest level – you cannot go up from this folder.

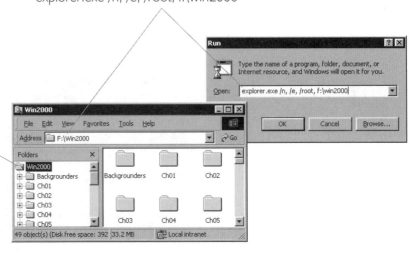

Accessing the Internet

This chapter looks at the functions Windows 2000 provides to help you establish an account, connect to the Internet, set up Internet mail and share your Internet connection over the Local Area Network.

Covers

Internet Connection Wizard | 68

Choosing your ISP | 70

Manual setup | 71

Internet over LAN | 73

Set up Internet mail | 74

Completing the definition | 76

Connecting | 77

Dial-up status | 78

Internet Explorer | 80

Home page | 81

Internet Connection Sharing | 82

Enabling ICS | 83

IP addressing | 84

ICS in action | 85

LAN status | 86

Chapter Four

Internet Connection Wizard

If you operate your PC in a stand-alone environment, you may use a modem and telephone line to dial the Internet Service Provider (ISP). If you are part of a workgroup, you may be able to share the connection defined on another user's PC. If you are part of a company network or domain, there may be a permanent Internet connection already in place, available for you to share.

When you start an Internet application, it checks to see if an Internet connection has been defined, and if not it will call up the wizard so you can set up your account.

Windows 2000 provides an Internet Connection Wizard (ICW) to help you specify the way that your Internet connection is provided, and how you want it configured.

There are a number of ways for you to start the wizard:

Connect to the Internet

- Double-click the Connect to the Internet icon that is added to the desktop during the initial Windows 2000 installation.

Internet Explorer

- Start Internet Explorer from the desktop, the Start menu or the Quick Launch bar, and it will determine if a connection needs defining.

Outlook Express

- Start Outlook Express from the Start menu or the Quick Launch bar, and it will take similar action.

Windows Update

- Select Windows Update from the Start menu and click one of the links offered.

These shortcuts to the wizard will be automatically removed when you have made the first connection. You will still be able to define additional connections (see page 71).

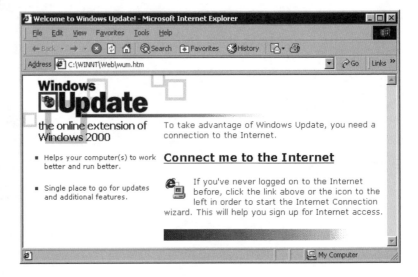

...cont'd

A modem must be installed and connected to the telephone line, since the wizard dials the server to collect data.

If the IC Wizard determines that the modem is not configured, it will run the Install New Modem wizard to configure your modem and request your dialling details, including your location (country and telephone area code).

Start the Internet Connection Wizard using any of the methods, and select to sign up for a new Internet account.

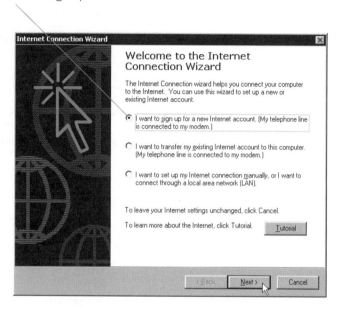

The modem then dials the referral server using a toll free 0800 number. This will download information about the ISPs available in your area.

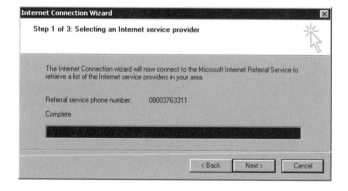

You can use the wizard to help you connect manually. See page 71.

This relies on ISPs being registered with Microsoft and, depending where you connect from, you may be told that there are "No offers available in your area at this time".

Choosing your ISP

The choice of ISPs and the order in which they are presented may change when you next sign on to the referral server.

The terms will vary between ISPs. Some are free, some charge a fee, and some offer a trial, so check your commitment before signing up.

Select the ISP that you want to consider, from the list on the left of the page. Details of the offer are shown on the right.

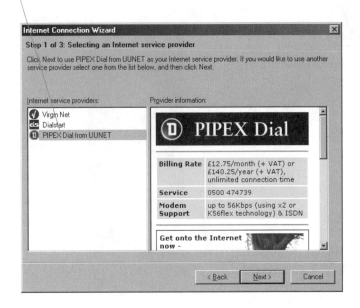

2 Follow the on-screen instructions to set up an account with the selected ISP and connect to the Internet.

If you selected the second ICW option, to transfer your existing account to the new system, you are shown the list of ISPs which will help you set up your account details.

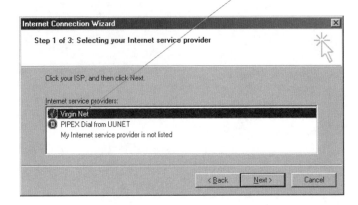

Manual setup

These steps show you what happens behind the scenes when you select the other ICW options.

If you selected the third ICW option (or if the ISP you want is not listed), you can enter the details physically.

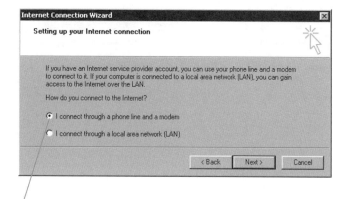

1   Select "I connect through a phone line and a modem" if you connect directly to the Internet, or select "I connect through a local area network (LAN)" if you are using a connection set up elsewhere on the LAN (see page 73).

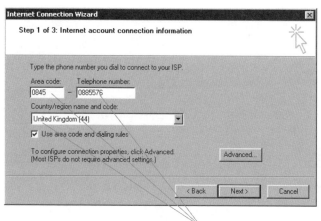

Some ISPs provide different phone numbers for different types of modem, for example V.90 or X2 modems.

2   For a modem connection, enter the area code, the telephone number and the country or region code. This information must be obtained from the ISP you have chosen. Make sure that the telephone number you enter is appropriate for the type of modem that you are using.

You must get these details exactly right or your connection will not be successful.

3 Enter the user name and password for your ISP account. You may need a prefix for the user name, such as UK/ or MSN/.

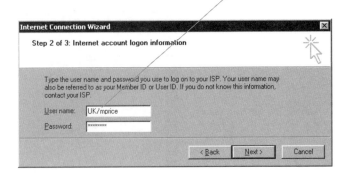

4 Provide a name for the connection. This is used in the dial-up networking tables to identify the connection and can be any freeform text that will remind you of the account.

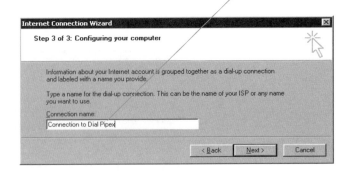

If you do want to use email, the ICW will help you set up the account and server definitions needed (see page 74).

5 If you do not want to use email with this ISP, select No. This completes the definition of the Internet dial-up connection and the ICW finishes (see page 76).

Internet over LAN

If you plan to connect through the Local Area Network (LAN), the setup is simpler, since the real definition takes place on the PC or server providing the connection.

See page 82 for details of setting up Internet Connection Sharing on a home or small office PC network.

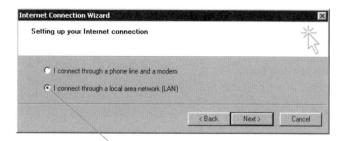

Select this to use a connection set up elsewhere on the Local Area Network, that is on a proxy server.

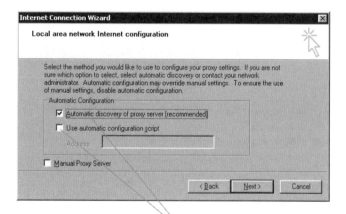

2 Select the method to use to configure your proxy settings. You may provide manual settings, or use an automatic configuration script supplied by your network administrator. If you are not certain which option to select, choose the Automatic Discovery option.

This completes the definition of the LAN Internet connection and the ICW finishes (see page 76).

Set up Internet mail

 Internet mail requires an email program. Windows 2000 includes a copy of Outlook Express, or you can use another program such as Eudora or Outlook 2002 from the Office suite.

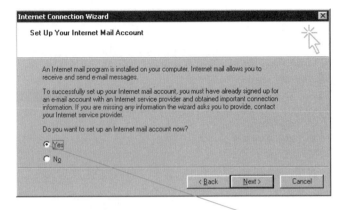

I If you want to use this ISP for Internet mail, select Yes. You must have details of the account and servers from the ISP.

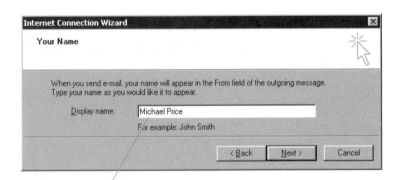

 *The display form is not critical, but you must enter the email address exactly as given, especially since the server could be case-sensitive.*

2 Enter your name as it should appear on your messages, and then enter the email address for your account, with the user name and the email server name.

3 Select the type of mail server that you will be using. This may be POP3, IMAP or HTTP.

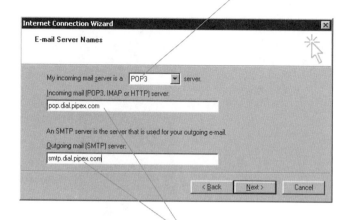

4 Enter the names for the mail servers for incoming and outgoing mail.

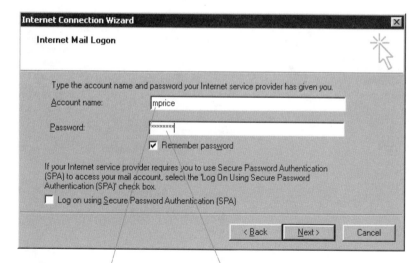

5 Enter the user name and the password for your account. Click the box if you want Windows to remember the password for you. Only do this if your PC is in a secure location or if you have specified that all users must logon with a password.

Completing the definition

When you have entered all the information requested, the wizard is ready to complete the definition. Click Finish.

 If you want to connect to the Internet to try out your account, click in the box.

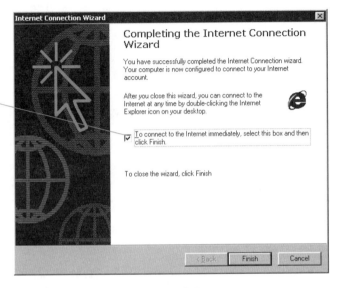

 You can select the connection to use, if you have more than one defined.

2 The dial-up connection will be started. Enter the password, unless you asked Windows to remember it for you. Click Connect and the modem will ring the number for your ISP and transfer the signon details. (By default, the connection will be tried up to ten times if a busy signal is received.)

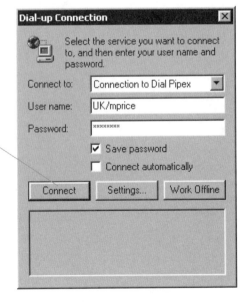

Connecting

Your signon details will be processed by the server and you will be connected to your ISP. The home page for the ISP, or the home page that you have chosen, is displayed.

Like many Web pages, this needs a screen resolution of 800 x 600 for best effect.

You can see that the connection is active because a Dial-up icon is added to the System tray. It shows when data is being transferred by flashing and changing colour. Hold the mouse pointer over the icon to see the data volumes sent and received and the connection speed.

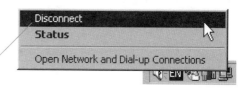

Select Status to see more information about the dial-up session (see page 78).

Right-click the icon to display the context menu. End the dial-up session by selecting Disconnect.

Dial-up status

You can view an ongoing report of the activity on the dial-up network.
There's also a Disconnect button.

1 Right-click the Dial-up icon and select Status (or double-click the icon).

The General tab shows the current status of the session, and the activity, including the effective compression rate as well as data volumes.

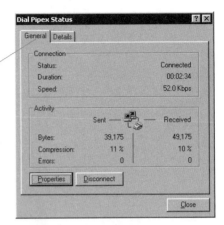

2 Click the Details tab to see more information about the session.

This shows the server type and the connection protocols being used. It also shows the IP addresses for the server and the client (your PC).

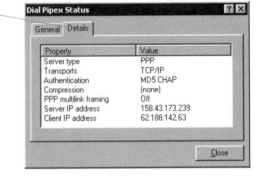

If the icon is hidden, you can still display the status by double-clicking the Dial-up icon in the Control Panel.

3 Click Properties on the General tab to see the settings for the current dial-up connection. This is where you can update the telephone number if it changes.

Clear the box if you do not want the Dial-up icon in the System tray.

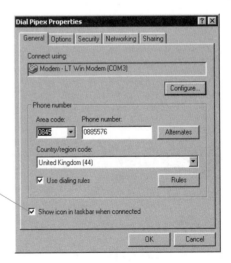

4 Right-click the Networking and Dial-up Connections icon in Control Panel and double-click your connection.

A brief status for the selected connection appears on the left side of the folder.

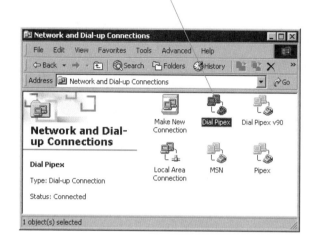

5 If the connection is currently active, the Status and Disconnect screen appears (see page 77).

6 If the connection is not currently active, the Dial screen appears. You can view the properties or dial the connection.

You will need to enter the password unless you have asked Windows to keep a record of it for you.

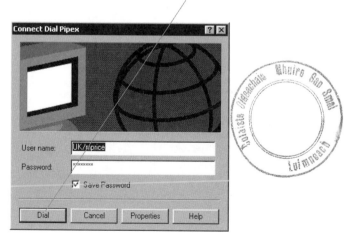

7 If there is another connection active, or if the modem is in use for another application, an error message is displayed.

Internet Explorer

When you create or transfer your ISP account using the ICW, it makes the changes necessary to your Internet Explorer settings. To see what information has been added:

If IE is already open, you can display the properties by selecting Tools, Internet Options.

1 Right-click the Internet Explorer icon on the desktop and select Properties.

2 Select the General tab to review or make changes to the cache settings.

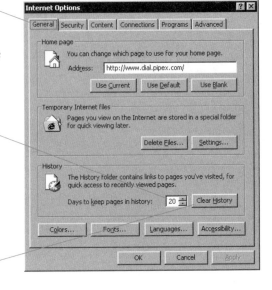

3 Specify for how many days you will keep pages in the temporary storage for offline viewing.

4 Click the Clear History button to empty the storage and start afresh.

In the Settings dialog, you can tell Internet Explorer how often to update the contents of stored Web pages.

5 Click the Settings button and move the slider to adjust the amount of temporary storage. By default, IE assigns 5% of your disk drive.

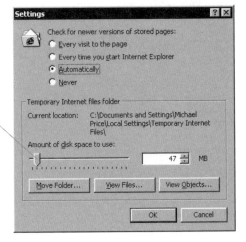

Home page

When you start Internet Explorer it displays the Web page specified in the IE properties. The same page is displayed when you click the Home button on the toolbar. The initial address for this Web page is defined when you set up your Internet account, but you can choose a different page:

1 While Internet Explorer is connected, select View, Internet Options and choose the General tab.

2 Click Use Current, to set the active page currently being displayed as the new Home page.

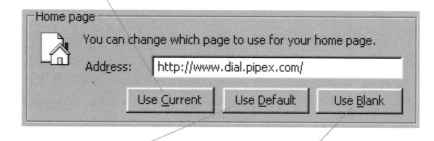

3 Click Use Default to restore the setup, or Use Blank for an empty page. This isn't very exciting, but does allow for the quickest Internet Explorer start-up.

4 Alternatively, type a URL address to select a particular Web page. This can be any page on the Web, including pages on your own Web space, or even a HTML file that you have created on your hard drive.

The default home page specified for Internet Explorer is: http://www.msn.com. In the UK this address is localised automatically and set to: http://msn.co.uk/default.asp. Your ISP usually provides a Home page – for example, Pipex uses the Welcome page: http://www.dial.pipex.com/.

Internet Connection Sharing

The Internet Connection Sharing feature is intended for use in a small office or home office.

With Windows 2000, you can connect several computers to the Internet through one connection. This capability is not restricted to company networks with servers. If you have two or three home PCs with network cards, one can connect to the Internet through a dial-up connection. By using Internet Connection Sharing, the other PCs can connect to the Internet at the same time, using only one phone line. Each connected PC can use any of the Internet services as if connected directly, such as Internet browsing, email, multiplayer gaming and chat sessions.

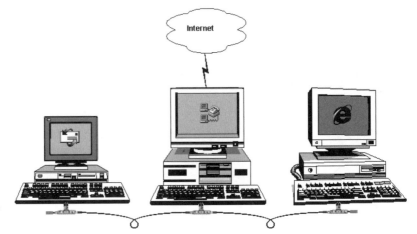

In order to configure ICS, you must be a member of the Administrators group.

The PC that has the dial-up connection provides network address translation, addressing, and name resolution services for all the PCs on the network. You may also need to configure some applications and services on this PC so that they will work properly across the Internet.

Do not use ICS if you are running the server edition of Windows 2000, or if your network has multiple Internet connections.

The Internet Connection Sharing feature is intended for use in a small office or home office where the network configuration and the Internet connection will be managed by the PC providing the shared connection. ICS assumes that this is the only Internet connection on the network.

You should not use this feature in an existing network with Windows 2000 servers or domain controllers, or on systems configured for static IP addresses.

Enabling ICS

To enable Internet Connection Sharing on the PC with the dial-up connection:

1 Open Network and Dial-up Connections from the Control Panel.

Network and
Dial-up
Connections

2 Right-click the connection you want to share, and then click Properties.

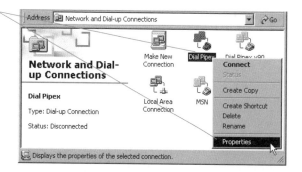

3 On the Sharing tab, select Enable Internet Connection Sharing for this connection.

If you want this connection to automatically dial up when another computer on your home network attempts to access external resources, select Enable on-demand dialing.

4 Click OK to save the changes and set up ICS.

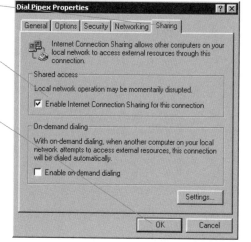

Any PC on the network that has been set up to use the LAN for Internet connection (see page 73) can now use the dial-up connection whenever it is active. Responses from the Internet will be redirected by ICS to the PC that originated the request.

IP addressing

When you enable ICS, the LAN adapter on the sharing PC is given a new static IP address. Existing TCP/IP connections may be lost, unless you have specified automatic IP address assignment.

To check the IP address setup and configuration on the PC:

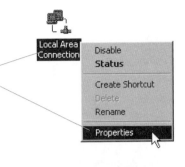

1 Right-click the LAN icon in the Network and Dial-up Connections folder and select Properties.

2 Select Show icon in taskbar when connected to place an icon in the System tray, just like the Dial-up Networking icon.

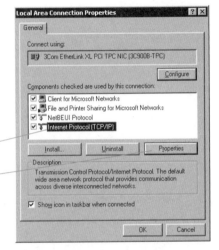

3 Select the Internet Protocol (TCP/IP) entry and click Properties.

4 If you have selected the automatic options for obtaining an IP address, there will be no problems when ICS is installed.

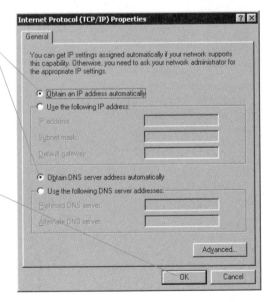

5 Click OK twice to apply any changes. For some changes, you may need to restart the system.

ICS in action

Note the bubble text that appears when the link (LAN or Dial-up) is enabled and the icon displayed.

1 The Dial-up connection shows in the System tray for the sharing PC, when the connection is active.

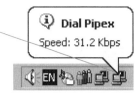

2 There is also an icon for the LAN connection.

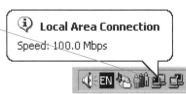

The LAN speeds may be different for the two PCs, if you are using a switched hub.

3 Only the LAN connection appears for the PC that will share the ICS connection.

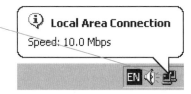

4 When you start Internet Explorer, it detects the Internet connection via the network link and displays the home page:

You can check progress and activity using the LAN status screen (see page 86).

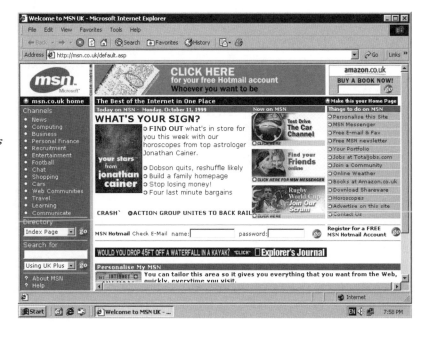

LAN status

 See Chapter 9 for more information on setting up and using a Local Area Network.

To check the status of the LAN connection, and detect the levels of activity:

1 Hover the mouse pointer over the LAN icon in the System tray, to see a brief Status note.

Local Area Connection 3
Speed: 100.0 Mbps
Sent: 3,964 packets
Received: 5,098 packets
EN

2 Alternatively, open the Networking and Dial-up Connections folder and select the LAN icon. This shows the status in brief.

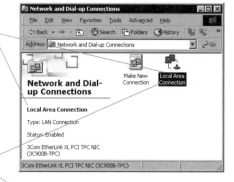

 The Status panel will also be displayed when you left-click the LAN icon in the System tray (or right-click and select Status).

3 Double-click the LAN icon (or right-click and select Status) to display more details of the connection.

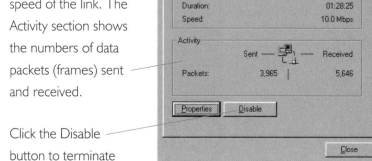

4 The Connection section shows the status, duration and speed of the link. The Activity section shows the numbers of data packets (frames) sent and received.

Local Area Connection Status ? X
General

Connection
Status: Connected
Duration: 01:28:25
Speed: 10.0 Mbps

Activity
Sent — Received
Packets: 3,965   5,646

Properties   Disable

Close

As well as ending an ICS link, clicking Disable will also disrupt any file and printer sharing.

5 Click the Disable button to terminate the LAN connection.

Installing Applications

This chapter looks at the different types of applications, including how to check that they are compatible, how to add them to your Windows system and how to manage and access them from the Start menu, Desktop or toolbars.

Covers

Certified for Windows | 88

Methods of installing | 90

Application migration | 91

Paint Shop Pro | 92

Visio | 94

Installing via Run | 96

Compressed applications | 97

What to watch for | 98

Adding/removing programs | 100

Legacy applications | 102

MS-DOS applications | 103

Managing the Start menu | 104

Chapter Five

Certified for Windows

Before you install an application under Windows 2000, check that it is supported to run in that environment, and if there are any limitations or restrictions in the functions when it runs in Windows 2000.

For more details of the Certified for Windows Logo programme, you should visit the Microsoft website at: `http://msdn.microsoft.com/winlogo/`

The first place to check is on the application's packaging. Many Windows applications carry the Certified for Microsoft Windows logo, which indicates that the application has passed compliance testing and made a logo licence agreement with Microsoft. The logo tells you that the application works to the standards of one or more of the available versions of Windows, as shown on the logo.

Compliance testing for Windows Certification is performed by VeriTest, an independent testing lab, and uses the latest released versions of the operating systems available at the time of testing, with the current service packs and the most recent version of Internet Explorer. For example:

*   Windows 2000

*   Windows NT 4, SP5, IE5

Applications may be certified to meet all the standards, or tested by the vendor as Ready for Windows 2000 operation, or the support may be planned in a future release.

*   Windows 98 Second Edition

*   Windows 95 OSR2, IE5

To check the status of your applications, review the list of compatible applications. Start at the website `http://www.microsoft.com/windows2000/professional`. Click the Compatibility link and select the Software option. This allows you to search by operating system type, application or company, and provides a three level rating for registered applications.

Search the directory for all applications that are compatible at one or other level with Windws 2000 Professional.

The search for compatible applications returns 2917 results, starting with Easy Web StoreFront which is flagged as Certified for Windows 2000

The guidelines for certification are very extensive, and give an insight into the strategy for Windows, and the strengths and weaknesses of particular versions. It is particularly interesting to identify the areas where the versions of Windows meet differing requirements. For example:

Applications should not put any shortcuts to help, documents or uninstall utilities in the Start menu.

Guideline	Win98	NT 4.0	Win2000
Don't read/write system files	-	X	X
Don't replace protected files	-	-	X
Use side-by-side components	X	-	X
Deny access gracefully	-	X	X
Obey system Group Policies	-	-	X
No extraneous shortcuts	X	X	X
Support multiple monitors	X	-	X
Upgrade to Win 2000	X	X	-

Applications should continue to function after an upgrade to Windows 2000 Professional, without reinstall.

These illustrate, for example, the greater emphasis on security and integrity in Windows NT and Windows 2000, versus the less secure but potentially more flexible Windows 98.

Methods of installing

There are a number of different ways of making applications available to your Windows 2000 system. The approach to use depends on what stage your upgrade has reached, and on the level of support in the application.

See Chapter 1 for notes on upgrading to Windows 2000.

1 If you have already installed applications under Windows 9x or Windows NT, upgrading to Windows 2000 may preserve the application with all its settings (see page 91).

2 If you need to re-install an existing application, or add a new application, insert the application CD into the drive (see page 92).

If AutoRun is enabled, the associated Setup program will run. Follow the on-screen instructions to install the application.

3 If AutoRun is not enabled, or if you are installing from diskette or the Network, you can run Add/Remove Programs (see page 94).

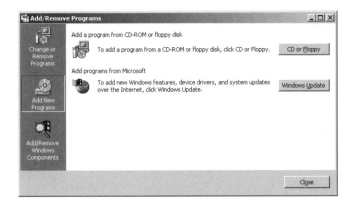

4 If the application has a nonstandard Setup program, you may need to run it directly. Select Start, Run and browse to the installation program and click OK (see page 96).

If you install a compression utility such as WinZip, this may be able to decompress and install an application in one operation.

5 If the application is supplied as a compressed file (e.g. .ZIP or .ARC), you will need to decompress it to locate the Setup program.

Application migration

The requirement for Windows certification is that previously installed applications will continue to function as before, with all preferences and privileges working after upgrade to Windows 2000 Professional. In practice, many Windows applications already comply. For example:

1 Start Opera under Windows 98 and select Help, About. Note that it detects Windows version 4.10:

2 Select the same program after Upgrade to Windows 2000. Note that it detects Windows NT version 5.0.

The application is aware of the change in operating system, and continues to function after the upgrade. However, it may not be able to use all the new capabilities.

To comply with the migration requirements, in the ideal case applications would use a single set of binaries and would not require different configurations on different operating systems. If the application uses features specific to a particular operating system, this will not be possible, so Windows 9x applications may need a migration DLL to make the changes needed – for example, to replace .VXD code with the equivalent Windows 2000 service.

If you have already upgraded to Windows 2000, and did not have the required migration DLL for an application, it will be unavailable and you must install it from scratch.

Paint Shop Pro

If you upgrade a system with Paint Shop Pro already installed, it continues to operate without reinstalling.

Paint Shop Pro 6 from Jasc Software carries the Designed for Windows logo for Windows NT and Windows 98. However, it makes such standard use of Windows facilities that you might expect it to run without problems under Windows 2000. To try installing the application:

PSP, in common with most Windows applications, invites you to register the product online or send in your registration card.

Insert the installation CD. The Setup program starts automatically. Click Install and follow the instructions.

Close all other programs before installation begins – see also page 98.

New entries appear at the end of the Programs list in the Start menu, but you can rearrange them.

2 The program files are copied, the application is configured and the Start menu is updated with a new folder.

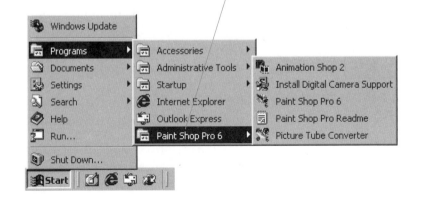

...cont'd

For more details on customising the Start menu and Desktop, see page 104.

3 Drag the entry to a new position and release the mouse button, to rearrange the sequence of entries.

4 Right-click the Start menu entry and select Sort by Name to put the menu into alphabetic order: folders first and then applications.

5 The first time you run Paint Shop Pro, it shows you the predefined file association list for you to accept or revise.

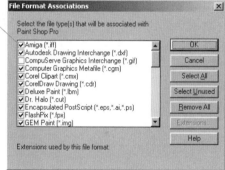

You may also want to select the File, Preferences option to change the default settings.

6 Remove unnecessary file extensions, and check for all the image types you will use with Paint Shop Pro.

7 The Registry is updated immediately and there's no need to restart the PC.

For a full-colour guide to Paint Shop Pro, see 'Paint Shop Pro 7 (Anniversary Edition) in easy steps'.

Paint Shop Pro 6 works perfectly well under Windows 2000 even though it is neither certified nor registered as ready for Windows 2000. However, there are some minor characteristics that may prevent it being certified without change. For example, the menu folder contains items which are inappropriate under the guidelines for the Windows logo programme.

Note that Paint Shop Pro 7 Anniversary Edition, released after Windows 2000, is certified for this operating system and does support it fully.

Visio

You can use the Control Panel's Add/Remove Programs option to install Windows applications.

1 Open the Control Panel, double-click Add/Remove Programs and then click the CD or Floppy button.

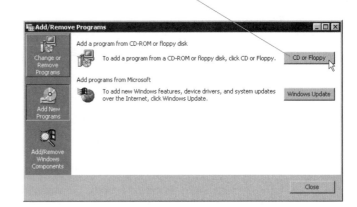

If the wizard fails to find the right program, you can browse to locate it yourself.

2 Insert the installation CD or diskette when prompted. The wizard should automatically detect the installation program.

Close all other programs before installation begins – see also page 98.

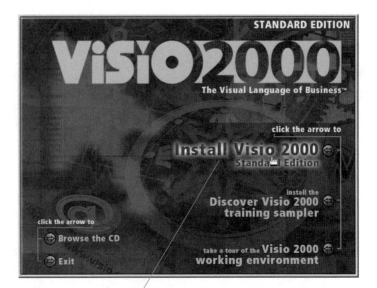

3 When the Setup program starts, choose the options to find out more about the application, or click Install Visio 2000.

...cont'd

Note that Visio uses Windows Installer as the basis for Setup, like Office XP and Windows 2000.

4 Allow the PC to be restarted if system files need to be installed or updated.

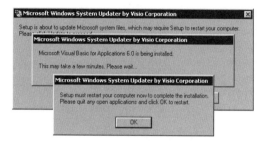

5 When the PC reboots, the application part of the installation starts. Follow the prompts to select the type of installation (Typical, Compact or Custom/Complete).

Again, you can choose to register over the Internet if you have a connection.

6 When Setup completes, there's no need to restart. The application appears on the Start, Programs menu immediately (and without all the extraneous shortcuts that some applications are fond of adding).

Installing via Run

1 Insert the Setup disk. Select Start, Run and Browse to locate the Setup program.

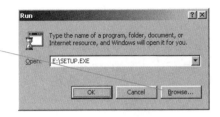

You can locate and execute the installation program directly. This is particularly useful when the application uses a nonstandard program name for the Install utility.

2 You may also start the program from the Command Prompt, or locate and double-click the program file icon.

3 Use this method to install the Phone Book Administrator from the \Valueadd folder on the Windows 2000 CD. Locate the PBAINST.EXE program, double-click it and click Yes.

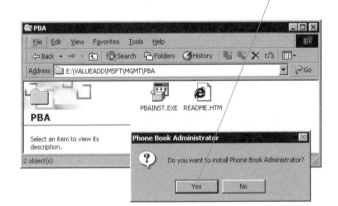

The Setup program may object to the Windows version because it is unexpected. In other cases, the installation may appear to succeed but the application may not operate correctly or may have some functions missing.

4 Not all applications will install under Windows 2000.

Compressed applications

When you receive an application to install, the files may be compressed and packaged in a single file. This may be a ZIP file (or another compressed file type), which requires a utility to expand and recreate the original files. The package could be a self-extracting .EXE file, which does not need a separate utility.

To install the application:

Run the .EXE file or process the ZIP file using, for example, PKUNZIP.EXE.

1 Create a program folder for the new application, usually in the Program Files folder, and Expand the file into the folder.

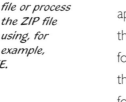

In some cases, the files generated are themselves installation files, so you may need to run SETUP.EXE (or a similar program).

2 If you install a Windows utility such as the shareware WinZip, it can be used to extract the files and run the Setup program, if this is required:

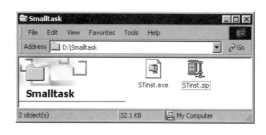

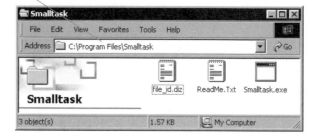

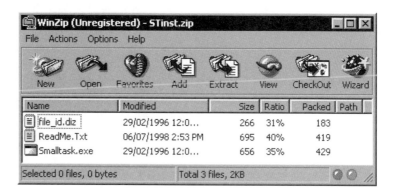

What to watch for

Antivirus programs are a particular concern because they monitor changes to system files etc.

1 You may be required to disable any antivirus software before installing. It's also better to stop all Windows applications.

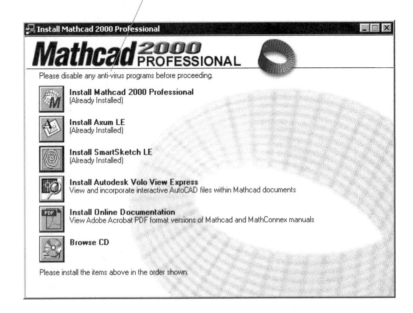

If there are several parts to an application, you may need to install them in a particular order.

You may need to install utilities such as the Acrobat Reader to access application documentation.

2 Some Setup programs ask for confirmation at every step, others use default values.

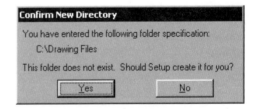

3 If you have multiple users on your PC, you must decide if a new program can be used by everyone.

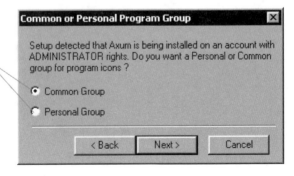

Your user level controls what powers you have.

Users with Standard authority can install some applications but have limits on utilities.

Restricted level or Guest users cannot install applications.

4 Select Shutdown and Logoff from the user name with administrative authority. Windows restarts at the Logon.

5 Logon as a user with Standard authority, and run the Setup program for a utility such as Quick View Plus. It will not install without permission because it changes system settings.

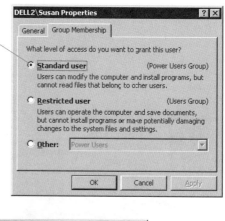

If you add a program as a standard user, it won't be available to other users on the system.

6 Install an ordinary application or game, in this case a demo of 5th Realm Tarot. This will install without problems.

If you logoff and logon as another user, you'll find that applications added by one user are not shown on the Start menu or Desktop for another user. However, all the programs will be on the Add/Remove Programs lists. The Administrator will be able to remove applications whoever added them, if they are considered unnecessary. Any applications added by the Administrator are available to all.

Adding/removing programs

Whichever way you add them, most applications will be recorded in the Add/Remove Programs list. To display this after installing several applications:

1   Open Control Panel, double-click Add/Remove Programs, and select the Change or Remove Programs button.

 Click the name in the list to get the details of size and usage for any program. There may also be a link showing support information.

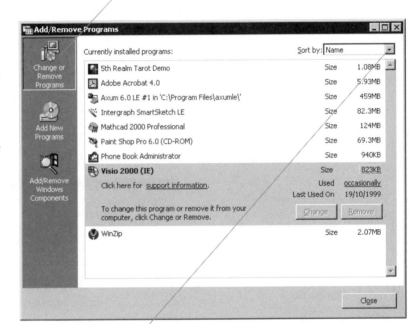

 The sort is always ascending, and the values for the field chosen will be displayed in the list.

2   Click the down-arrow and select to sort by the name, the size, the frequency of use or the date last used.

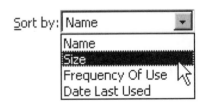

3   Windows measures the number of times a program has been used in the past thirty days, and classes it as frequently, occasionally or rarely used. These ratings will be revised the next time you visit the list, if the usage patterns change.

Continuing the example with Acrobat Reader:

The Change or Remove features offered depend on the individual application.

1 Open Add/Remove Programs, select the program list and click the name of the application.

2 Click Change to run the Setup program or Remove to run the Uninstall program for the application.

You will usually need the Setup CD to run Change or Change/ Remove.

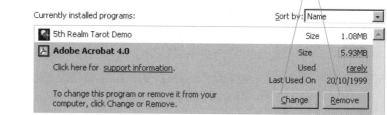

3 Click Change/Remove to run the single program, which could be Setup or Uninstall.

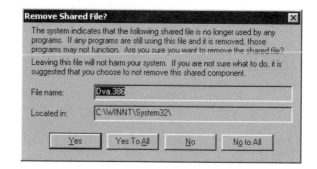

It is normally OK to remove files if they are not otherwise used, but – if in doubt – leave them on the hard disk.

Note that when an application program is removed, the entries on the Start menus for all users are also removed.

4 You may be asked whether you want to remove library files that are no longer in use:

Legacy applications

Legacy applications for the PC refer to older 16-bit applications designed to run under a different operating system such as MS-DOS or Windows 3.x.

Windows 2000 provides support for legacy applications by emulating the operating environment for which they were designed. The subsystems provided within the operating system include:

OS/2 subsystem

This runs 16-bit character-based OS/2 applications and emulates OS/2 version 1.3. It does not support applications designed for OS/2 version 2 or OS/2 Warp.

POSIX subsystem

This runs applications designed for the portable operating system for UNIX.

Windows 2000 runs 16-bit Windows applications in one multi-threaded NTVDM, so they share the same address space. However, there is an option to run an application in separate memory space.

NTVDM (NT Virtual DOS Machine)

This emulates an Intel 486 PC. Each 16-bit MS-DOS application runs as a separate process in its own address space, so that a failed application won't affect the rest of the system. There's a Win16 version of the NTVDM which supports 16-bit Windows applications.

Win32 subsystem

To complete the set, there is also a subsystem for all the normal, 32-bit Windows applications.

The Windows 2000 approach to running legacy applications allows pre-emptive multitasking for all applications, not just for Win32 applications as in Windows 98. It also preserves the robust and secure environment that has been the hallmark of NT systems. To install a legacy application:

1   Select Start, Run. Type the path to the Setup or Install program for the application and click OK.

2   If there is no explicit installation program, copy the program files to a suitable subfolder in C:\Program Files.

3   If desired, add an entry for the program in the Start menu.

MS-DOS applications

A program information file (PIF) is created when you create a shortcut to a MS-DOS program.

PIFs allow you to set default properties such as font size, screen colours and memory allocation.

The properties for a MS-DOS program are contained in the associated Program Information File (PIF). A PIF file will be created automatically when you add a MS-DOS program to the Start menu.

1 Select Start, Settings, Taskbar & Start menu. Click the Advanced tab and click Add.

2 Enter the program path and name. Auto Complete helps by showing possible values.

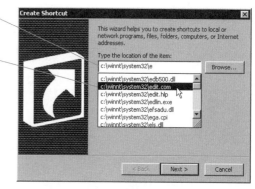

3 Right-click the new Start menu entry and select Properties.

You can also adjust options for MS-DOS programs by right-clicking the Title bar and selecting Properties.

For example, you can turn QuickEdit off or on, and use the mouse to select menu commands or to copy and paste text.

4 Click a tab to make changes. For example, click Screen and choose Window or Full-screen as needed.

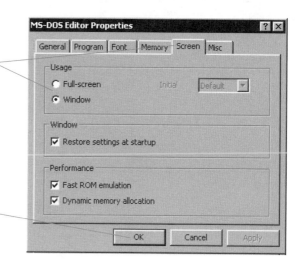

5 Click OK to save and apply the changes.

Managing the Start menu

When you install an application, Setup creates a new entry in the Start menu. You are usually offered a choice of folder, but the default will normally be to add a program or folder entry into the Programs folder.

After installation, you can remove, resequence or rename the entries. To customise entries in Start menu folders:

1 Select Start, Settings, Taskbar & Start Menu and click Advanced.

2 Click Add, Remove or Re-sort, or click the Advanced button to display the Start menu in Windows Explorer.

3 The changes are targeted at the Start menu for the logged on user.

To make changes to the Start menu that will become available to every user:

There is little protection for the contents of the Start menu – in practice, any user may make changes to the shortcuts of any other user.

1 Logon as the Administrator, right-click the Start button and select Explore All Users.

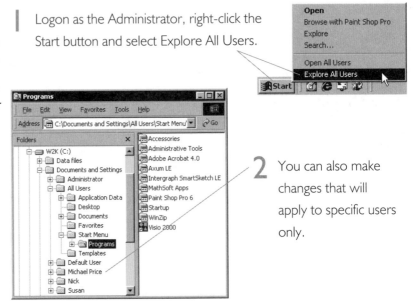

2 You can also make changes that will apply to specific users only.

Customising the Layout

You can change the way that the Windows 2000 Desktop and menus appear and modify the way that it operates, to suit your own preferences.

Covers

Default Desktop | 106

Tile wallpaper | 108

Active Desktop | 109

Colour and resolution | 110

Appearance | 112

Screensavers | 114

Changing frequency | 116

Other options | 117

Start menu and Taskbar | 118

Adding My Computer | 120

Customising the Taskbar | 121

Taskbar toolbars | 122

Other customisations | 124

Chapter Six

Default Desktop

The way Windows 2000 was set up will affect the look of the Desktop and Start menu, but what you see can be changed.

Your PC may have Windows 2000 Professional already pre-installed by the supplier or by your system administrator. If you have an existing Windows system such as Windows 98 or Windows NT installed, you could purchase the Windows 2000 upgrade to install over the current system. You can still use the upgrade even if you want to start with a clean slate – you'd format your drive before installing the update.

All the different ways of adding Windows 2000 will affect the appearance and content of the Desktop, Start menu and folder organisation, but you do not have to settle for the default settings that you inherit with the system. You can make changes and turn things around into the form and layout that suit you best.

If you have accepted all the defaults, you may have a Desktop that looks like this:

Features of the Windows 2000 interface which are worthy of note include:

- *Shortcuts added to the Desktop by Windows applications*
- *Folders using the Web style format with a background image and notes, and;*
- *A Desktop surface coloured but otherwise left uncluttered*

- Size 640 x 480 pixels (the lowest resolution) with true colour resolution (32-bit).

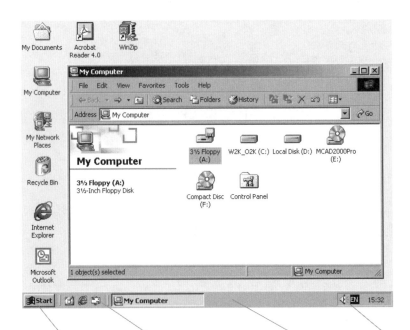

- Start button, Quick Launch toolbar, Taskbar and the System tray.

The Desktop is synonymous with the display device, and is controlled by the Display Properties.

In Windows 2000, you'll find a range of options for setting up the PC to suit the way you work and to match your personal preferences. The options for making changes can be found in the Control Panel but there are usually several other ways to access the change facilities.

For example, if you want to make changes to the Desktop appearance, you can:

If several people share the same PC, each user can customise the PC without changing another user's settings, since Windows 2000 will automatically save changes to the settings for the current user and reactivate those settings at the next logon.

1 Right-click the Desktop, select Active Desktop, Customise My Desktop and open Display Properties at the Web tab.

2 Right-click the Desktop and select Properties. (These will open at the Background tab).

3 Double-click Display in Control Panel, to open Properties (at the Background tab).

Display

4 Select a background picture from the list of wallpapers.

5 Click Browse to locate an image file to use as wallpaper.

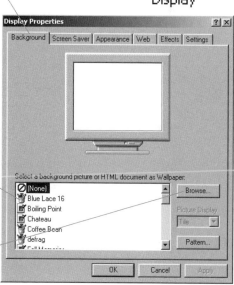

Tile wallpaper

Windows lets you tile or stretch your wallpaper.

Background pictures may be file types: .BMP, .DIB, .GIF or .JPG. You can also set a .HTM page as your wallpaper. (The Center, Tile, and Stretch options are unavailable for .HTM backgrounds.)

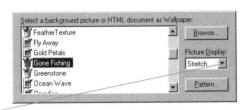

1 When you've chosen a background picture, click the down arrow in Picture Display and choose Stretch to fill the Desktop with a single copy of the image.

2 Change the setting to Tile to fill the Desktop with multiple copies of the image.

3 Choose Center to place a single copy of the image centred on the Desktop.

If you use Center with an image that is smaller than the Desktop, you can fill the rest of the space with a pattern.

To set or change the pattern:

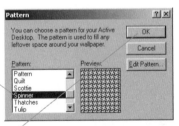

The Pattern button is not available if you Tile or Stretch the background picture.

1 Choose the Pattern tab and select the desired pattern. Click Edit Pattern to make changes.

2 Click OK to replicate the pattern around the centred image.

Active Desktop

When you select a .JPG image or a .HTM page, you need to switch to the Active Desktop.

1 If you are using the default Desktop, right-click it and select Active Desktop, Show Web Content. If ticked, it is enabled already.

2 Select a .HTM page or a .JPG image – e.g. select Paradise with Stretch. Then click OK.

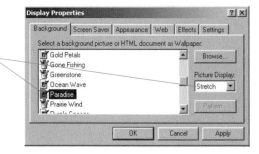

You can have two images – one for the Active Desktop and one for the normal Desktop – and switch between them using the Desktop Context menu to enable or disable Web content.

3 If you haven't yet enabled Web content, it will offer to do this for you.

4 The Desktop is displayed with the Web content activated:

You can hide the Desktop icons as well, using the Desktop Context menu.

Colour and resolution

If you have a 256-colour setting and open several applications in overlapping windows, you'll find that the colours in some windows get distorted when you switch to another window.

Monitors will display up to 16 million colours, depending on the amount of memory on the display adapter card and the screen resolution you have selected. The minimum required for Windows and Internet operation is 256 colours. Since different applications may specify different palettes of 256 colours, you may prefer to select a higher setting. However, the higher the setting, the more processor resources will be used.

To change the number of colours displayed on the monitor:

1 Open Display Properties and click the Settings tab.

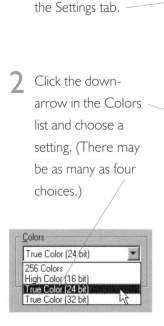

The list will show all the options available for your installed hardware and the current screen size.

2 Click the down-arrow in the Colors list and choose a setting. (There may be as many as four choices.)

A High Color setting will display more than 65,000 colours. A True Color setting will allow over 16 million colours.

3 Click OK to change the settings and close Properties, or Apply to see the effect without closing.

4 You must confirm the change or it will be cancelled.

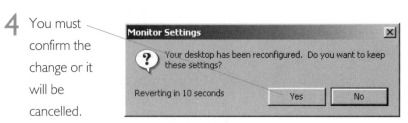

...cont'd

Low resolution makes the items on your Desktop appear large, while higher resolution increases the effective size of your Desktop but makes the individual items appear smaller.

The Settings tab also allows you to change the screen resolution. This is measured in pixels (picture elements), and the choices offered depend on the adapter card memory and capabilities, but may be further constrained by the monitor capabilities.

To adjust the screen resolution:

1   Click and drag the slider to the right to increase the size, and to the left to decrease the size.

2   Release the slider when the required resolution is selected, and click OK or Apply.

If you are using multiple monitors, click the monitor icon that represents the monitor that you want to adjust. The Extend my Windows Desktop onto this monitor check box must be selected to change the settings for that monitor.
You can specify the colour setting and the resolution for each installed monitor individually.

640 x 480 pixels

800 x 600 pixels

As with colour changes, you must confirm that the change has been successful or it will be reversed, as a precaution against unsupported configurations.

1024 x 768 pixels

1600 x 1200 pixels

Appearance

You may need to try out several sets of screen resolutions, system fonts and display schemes (see the facing page) to find out which combination suits you best.

The paradox of screen resolution is that higher settings improve the image because of the fine pixel size, but the icons and fonts get harder to read because they are smaller. However, you can make changes to compensate.

To use larger system display fonts:

1 Open Display Properties, select the Settings tab and click Advanced. Click the General tab. You can then select Large Fonts.

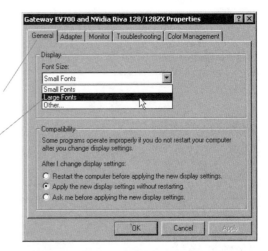

The font size you specify on the General tab affects all monitors if you have more than one. You can change font settings for individual window items on the Appearance tab, but your choices reflect the size of the system display font you specified.

2 If you choose Other instead, you can select a percentage (multiples of 25%). Click on the ruler and drag right to increase or left to decrease the size of the font.

3 You'll have to restart the PC, so the font files can be copied and the change put into effect.

You can change individual elements of the windows, menus and scrollbars, adjusting settings such as colour and font style or size.

There are over twenty predefined display schemes, from Brick to Windows Classic. Many have several versions e.g. small, large and extra large.

1 Open Display Properties at the Appearance tab and select one of the predefined colour and font schemes.

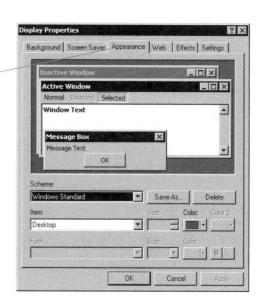

Click Save As and type a name for the amended scheme, which will be added to the Schemes list.

2 To customise the selected scheme, choose items and modify the settings.

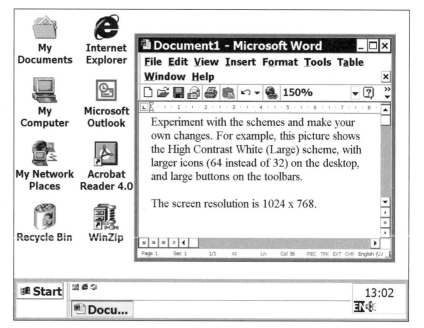

This shows a modified example of the High Contrast White (large) scheme on a high resolution screen.

Screensavers

Windows 2000 comes complete with a dozen screensavers, to decorate the display while the keyboard and mouse are idle.

To set or change a screensaver:

A screensaver is a moving picture or pattern that appears on your screen when you have not used the mouse or keyboard for a specified period of time. It dates from the days of high persistence phosphor monitors, where a static image could get burned into the display. No longer a necessity, it is now used for security and entertainment purposes, and is one of the most popular add-on applications.

1 Open Display Properties at the Screen Saver tab and click the down-arrow to display the list.

2 To see what the selected screensaver does, click Preview.

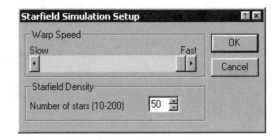

3 Specify the idle time before the screensaver starts. To view the other options for a screensaver, click Settings.

4 For the Starfield Simulation for example, you can specify the Warp speed and the starfield density.

5 The screensaver will automatically start when your PC keyboard and mouse have been idle for the number of minutes specified, though the processor may be busy.

To clear the screensaver after it has started, move your mouse or press any key. The screensaver immediately closes and the windows are re-displayed.

Attaching your logon password to your screensaver helps protect your system while you are away from the PC, without you having to logoff.

To enable password control with your screensaver:

Your screensaver password is the same as your logon

password.

Open Display Properties, select the Screen Saver tab, click Password protected and press Apply.

Only you can restart the current session. Other users will not be able to

access the system.
Your Administrator, however, can logon, causing the current session to be ended.

This will lock your PC when the screensaver is activated. When you begin working again you will be prompted to type your password to unlock it.

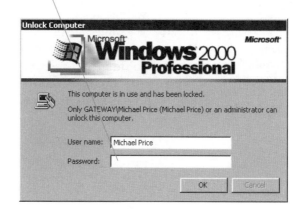

Note that if you start the screensaver from a shortcut to the .SCR file, or from the .SCR file itself, password protection will not be enabled until after the specified delay period, unlike the Windows 98 situation, where the protection is immediate.

Shortcut to
ssstars

Changing frequency

To change the refresh frequency for your monitor:

In order to maintain the image, the screen must be updated continually. The refresh rate is the number of times per second that every pixel on the screen is rewritten.

The default for Windows 2000 is 60 Hertz (this is too low for comfort).

1 Open Display Properties, select the Settings tab and click Advanced.

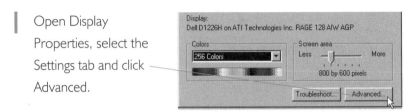

2 Select the Monitor tab and click the down-arrow in Refresh Frequency to choose a rate.

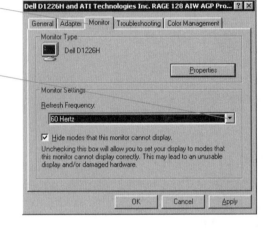

The default refresh frequency in Windows 2000 is only 60 Hertz, although your monitor will most likely support a higher setting. If your monitor is a plug-and-play device, Windows 2000 will automatically display only those rates applicable to the current screen resolution and colour setting. If you have a monitor that is unknown to Windows 2000, check the maker's documentation for the resolutions and refresh rates supported.

A higher refresh frequency reduces any flicker on your screen, but choosing a setting that is too high for your monitor can make your display unusable and cause damage to your hardware.

If possible select a rate that is 72 Hertz or greater, to get the minimum rate for comfort.

3 With a Dell 19" monitor attached to an ATI AIW adapter, there are nine options at 640 x 480. There are only two options offered at 1600 x 1200.

56 Hertz
60 Hertz
70 Hertz
72 Hertz
75 Hertz
85 Hertz
90 Hertz
100 Hertz
120 Hertz

60 Hertz
70 Hertz

Other options

The Control Panel provides further ways to personalise your PC. Folder Options allow you to change the way in which folder items are presented.

1 Select Folder Options from Control Panel or from the folder Tools menu.

There is also a folder customisation wizard which allows you to create templates and add backgrounds and comments for individual folders.

See page 29 for information about files and folders.

2 Select View, Customise this Folder and select the template. You can edit this to make further changes if you wish.

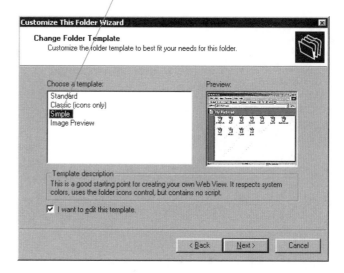

Note that Windows 2000 offers the following sound schemes:

- *No sounds*
- *Windows default*
- *Utopia sound*

You can select a sound scheme for your PC so that you will receive particular audio cues for specific events such as the arrival of email.

3 Select Sounds and Multimedia from the Control Panel. Select the Sounds tab then choose a predefined sound scheme.

Start menu and Taskbar

The size and style of the font used for the Start menu can be changed using Display Properties.

The Start menu and Taskbar are the most used elements, so Windows 2000 lets you customise their appearance and the way they work. To make changes:

1 Click Start, Settings, Taskbar & Start Menu. Alternatively, right-click the Taskbar and select Properties.

2 Always on top ensures that the Taskbar is visible, even with maximised windows.

Always on top is still needed when you use Auto hide, so the Taskbar will reappear in a visible location.

3 With Auto hide, the Taskbar is hidden until the mouse pointer is at the edge of the screen.

4 Shows small instead of large icons in the Start menu.

The Show small entry applies to the first level only – other menu levels always have small icons.

5 Puts a digital clock in the System tray. Hover over the clock for the date.

6 Personalised menus reduce the size of the Programs menu by hiding the least used entries. (Click the menu chevron to reveal the full menu.)

...cont'd

Windows 2000 will remember which entries you use most often and hide the others away to reduce the menu size.

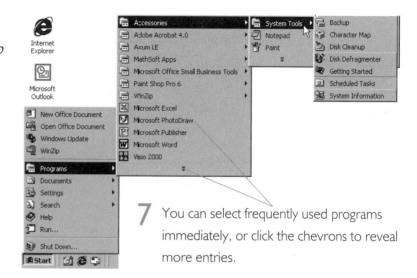

7 You can select frequently used programs immediately, or click the chevrons to reveal more entries.

8 To change settings, click Advanced and select or clear items to turn them on or off.

See pages 92–93 for examples of adding and moving shortcuts to the Start menu.

Add the Administrative Tools menu to the Programs menu.

Add Favorites to the Start menu.

Opening a folder as a list makes it easy to select items. You can right-click the menu entry and select Open to see the contents in a window.

Add a Logoff command to the Start menu.

Display the Control Panel, My Documents, Network Dial-up or Printers folder in a list instead of a window.

Display the Programs menu in a scrolling list instead of columns.

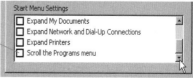

6. Customising the Layout | 119

Adding My Computer

There's no explicit option in the Start menu settings, but you can add the My Computer folder as a cascading list.

The contents of the drives (and the Control panel) in My Computer will be displayed in lists if you add My Computer to the Start menu.

1 Click the My Computer icon with the left mouse button, drag it onto the Start button and release it there.

2 The folder is added as an entry near the top of the first level of the Start menu.

This link to Control Panel will open as a list whatever you set in Start menu properties for the Settings shortcut to Control Panel.

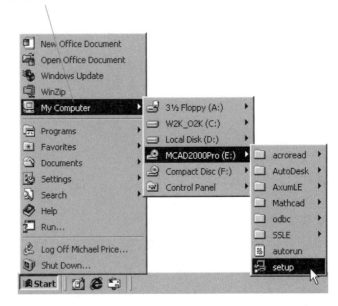

You can drag-and-drop any shortcut, or folder containing shortcuts, onto the Start button, to create a cascading menu.

3 You can add other folders to the Start menu. Create a folder with some shortcuts, e.g.: Word Apps.

4 Drag and hold the folder over the Start button for a couple of seconds and the menu expands. Pause over folder entries, and the next level expands, so you can navigate down to lower menu levels before dropping the folder.

Customising the Taskbar

The Taskbar is the home for the Start button, the Quick Launch toolbar, the System tray and buttons for active programs and open windows (see page 37).

The Taskbar appears by default at the bottom of the Desktop, one row high and always visible. You can resize or hide it, move it to the sides or top of the Desktop, and add other toolbars.

To resize the Taskbar:

Click and drag the top (or outer) edge of the Taskbar and release it at the height (or width) required.

To hide the Taskbar, modify the properties (see page 118).

To move the Taskbar:

You can temporarily hide the Taskbar by dragging the top edge down. To redisplay the Taskbar, drag the edge back up.

Click an empty area on the Taskbar, drag the Taskbar to a different location on the Desktop, and resize it as needed.

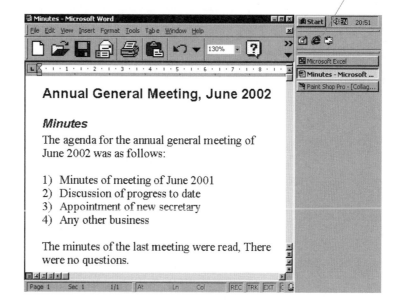

The display area for applications is adjusted to match, when the Taskbar is resized or repositioned.

Taskbar toolbars

To add toolbars onto the Taskbar:

A tick means that the toolbar is already enabled. Click it to reverse the setting.

1 Right-click an empty area on the Taskbar, select Toolbars and then click the toolbar you want to use.

Note that you can choose from the following predefined toolbars:

• *Quick Launch*
• *Address*
• *Link, and;*
• *Desktop*

2 Right-click the header bar on the toolbar to customise it e.g. deselect Show Text or Show Title, or choose View, Large.

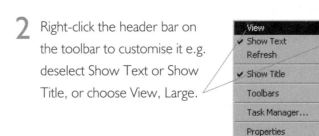

3 Resize the Taskbar if necessary (see page 121).

You can resize the toolbar you have generated, or move it to another location on the Taskbar by clicking on the header bar and dragging it to the left or right.

4 Drag the toolbar from the Taskbar to the Desktop to create a floating toolbar, or dock it on an edge of the display.

You can also define a new, custom toolbar for the Taskbar.

5 To create a new toolbar based on a folder of shortcuts, right-click the Taskbar, select Toolbars, New Toolbar and locate the shortcut folder.

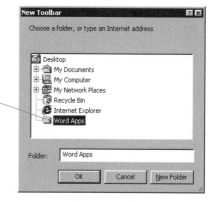

6 The contents are added as a toolbar. You can move, resize, customise or float the custom toolbar just like any of the predefined toolbars.

If you have floated or docked a toolbar, right-click an empty space on that toolbar to display the properties.

7 The new toolbar is added to the list of toolbars displayed when you right-click the Taskbar and select Toolbars.

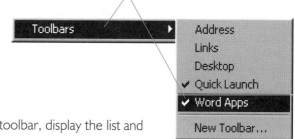

8 To remove a toolbar, display the list and reselect an enabled entry (with a tick) to remove the tick and the toolbar. Note that you'll have to recreate a custom toolbar to redisplay it.

Other customisations

1 Open Regional Options in Control Panel to adjust the presentation style for date, time, numbers and currency information (see page 50).

2 Open Keyboard to change the cursor blink rate, the character repeat rate, the input locale or the languages available (see page 53).

3 Open Mouse to change the button configuration, adjust the double-click and motion speed or switch to single-click selection (see page 54).

To change the appearance of your mouse pointer:

A pointer scheme is any combination of pointers used on your Desktop. You can customise a number of pointers and then save them as a new scheme by clicking Save As. The new scheme will be added to the list.

1 Open Mouse and click the Pointers tab to select a scheme and change the appearance of all the classes of pointers. Windows 2000 has twenty pointer schemes, ranging from variations on the Windows standard to the splendid Dinosaur scheme.

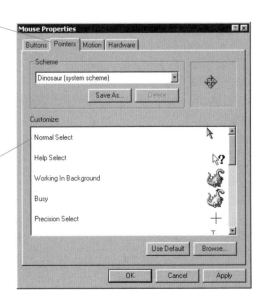

2 To change an individual pointer, select it in the list of specific tasks, click Browse and then double-click the name of the new pointer.

Exchanging Information

This chapter explores the ways in which Windows 2000 enables applications to share and update data, in particular the facilities offered through the Clipboard and Resource Kit utilities that enhance it. The roles of OLE, ActiveX and related technologies are also discussed.

Covers

Sharing information | 126

Using the Clipboard | 127

Viewing the ClipBook | 128

Pasting text | 130

Text to Paint | 132

Cut and paste images | 133

Add images to text | 134

Paste to Notepad | 136

Cut and Paste | 137

Drag-and-Drop | 138

Clip from Command Prompt | 139

Embedded objects | 140

Linking objects | 142

OLE Registration | 144

Chapter Seven

Sharing information

The most significant aspect of the Windows environment is the way it allows applications to exchange information. The primary support is provided by the Clipboard capability. This is an area of memory set aside to hold copies of application data in various formats.

The term 'document' is used in its generic Windows sense to represent any formatted information whether a textual report, an image, spreadsheet or presentation.

Documents in Windows applications can contain objects of more than one type, so a Word document, for example, can contain bitmaps and spreadsheet information. Such documents are referred to as compound documents. The Clipboard can be used to help build these, since it can handle all the types of data that you find in Windows applications, and will pass the data to an application in the format that it expects and is able to process. The data is exchanged through the Clipboard, using copy and paste operations. The transferred data can become part of the new document, or remain as a data object and retain its original identity.

The Office applications have their own Clipboard which cooperates with the Windows Clipboard.

The Clipboard can handle only one item at a time, making it hard to assemble collections of extracts. Any item added to the Clipboard can be reused to add it to other documents, but only until the next piece of data arrives in the Clipboard, and the contents are lost when the system shuts down. Windows 2000 extends the facilities of the Clipboard with the ClipBook viewer, and there are many third party products designed to enhance Clipboard operations.

The Clipboard does not provide support for maintaining the compound document, except implicitly when you use it to rebuild the document, copying and pasting new versions of the transferred objects whenever they change.

The Windows Help system with its Internet URLs provides an example of ActiveX in operation.

Windows does provide control over data exchanges and update, with technologies such as Dynamic Data Exchange (DDE), Object Linking and Embedding (OLE) and the underlying Component Object Model (COM). These have been extended into Distributed Component Object Model (DCOM) for sharing across networks, and ActiveX for sharing over the Internet. However, you do not have to be concerned with all these standards, since this is all handled automatically by Windows when you utilise the data exchange facilities provided.

Using the Clipboard

The Clipboard is the easiest way to transfer information, whether it is from one application to another or from one part of a document to another. However, you still have a number of options and alternatives to choose from, and these will vary depending on which application acts as the source and which as the target for the information.

The following sections trace some of the paths that a piece of data may take as it passes through the Clipboard, to illustrate the options.

The source text uses Arial, Times New Roman and Lucida Handwriting fonts, plus bold and italic type styles. There are tabs inserted to create the columns.

1 Load WordPad and open the source document, which in this case contains formatted text in a mixture of sizes and fonts, and arranged into columns.

Winkey	Effect
Win	*Display or hide the Start menu.*
Win+D	*Minimise or restore all windows.*
Win+E	*Open My Computer.*
Win+F	*Search for a file or folder.*
Win+R	*Open the Run dialog box.*
Win+Tab	*Switch between open items.*
Win+U	*Open Utility Manager.*
Win+Break	*Display the System Properties sheet.*
Win+F1	*Display Windows 2000 Help.*

Table prepared by Michael Price

2 Click Edit, Select All to highlight the text, and then click the Copy button to transfer the text to the Clipboard.

You can highlight text by clicking and dragging, or by clicking the start point, holding Shift and clicking the end point.

3 You can also copy highlighted text by clicking Edit, Copy or by pressing Ctrl+C.

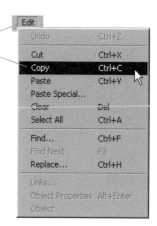

Viewing the ClipBook

The Clipboard Viewer used in Windows 98 is replaced by the ClipBook Viewer in Windows 2000.

1 Click Start, Run. Type CLIPBRD.EXE and click OK. Now view the contents of the Clipboard using the ClipBook Viewer:

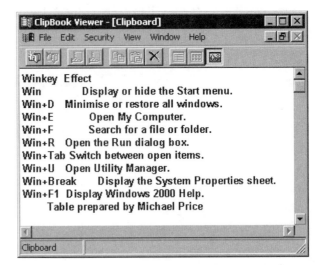

The copied data exists in the Clipboard in several formats, as shown on the View list. Formats that are greyed are not applicable to the current data object in the Clipboard.

2 Click View from the Menu bar to see the list of format styles supported. Click a format to see how it will appear.

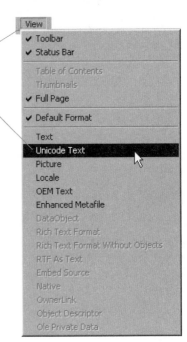

Normally, the Default Format is the best option, but you can view the contents of the Clipboard in any of the available styles, in this case Text, Unicode Text (which is the default format), Picture, Locale, OEM Text and Enhanced Metafile.

There are a number of other formats that may sometimes be used, depending on the application data types.

...cont'd

3 Select Window, Local ClipBook to switch from the Clipboard view.

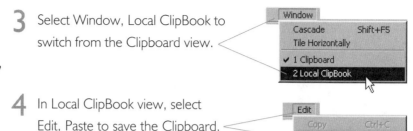

4 In Local ClipBook view, select Edit, Paste to save the Clipboard.

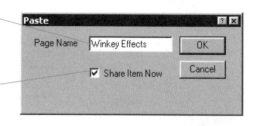

5 Name the ClipBook page. Select this box if you want to share the page, and click OK.

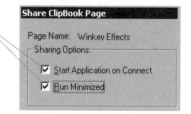

6 Select the sharing options you need, and select the boxes to allow programs to run automatically.

7 The Clipboard item is added to the ClipBook. Click the toolbar buttons to select:

Connect or Share.

Copy, Paste or Delete.

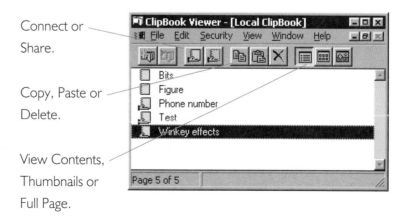

View Contents, Thumbnails or Full Page.

Pasting text

The text in the Clipboard can be pasted into another part of the same WordPad document, or it can be inserted into another WordPad or other Windows document.

I Load a second copy of WordPad to open a new document which will be the target or destination. Select Edit, Paste to add the text to the target document.

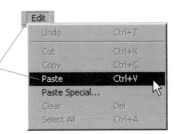

2 The text becomes part of the document, just as if you'd typed it, and you can reformat it or make changes.

With the default option, the text appears exactly as in the source document with all of the font formatting and tabs.

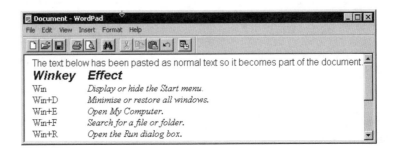

3 If you want the text to remain fixed, select Edit, Undo to remove the last copy and then select Edit, Paste Special.

4 Choose Picture (Metafile) as the type of object and click OK. The text is inserted as a picture which you cannot directly modify.

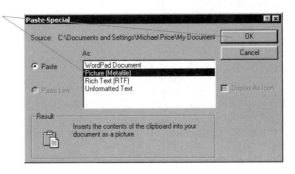

...cont'd

The inserted Metafile text is just an image in the new document.

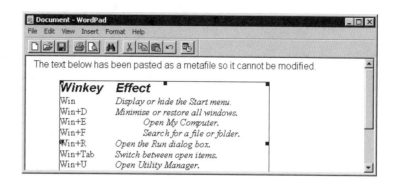

Another way to insert the text yet keep it separate from the rest of the document is to use the WordPad object format.

The icon acts as a placeholder in the document. The text can be changed, but it remains a separate element in the document.

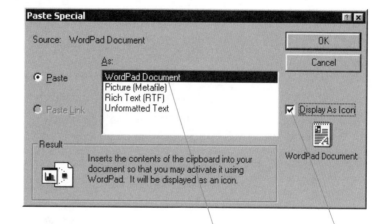

5 Select Edit, Paste Special, pick WordPad Document and click Display As Icon.

If you make any changes, select File and then choose Update Document to change the object, or Save Copy As to create a new document.

6 To make changes to the embedded text, double-click the icon to open the inserted text object in a separate WordPad window.

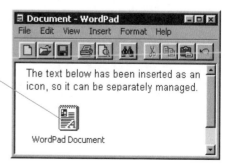

Text to Paint

The same WordPad data from the Clipboard can be transferred to the Paint application.

Start the Paint program and select Edit, Paste to add the text to the new image file.

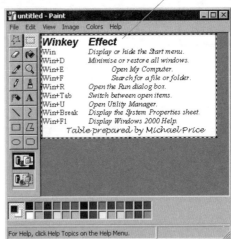

The text appears formatted as in WordPad but this is a bitmap image and so it cannot be edited as text. This is just a screen snapshot, so image quality could be poor with small font sizes or lower display resolutions.

If you want to edit the text when you have added it to your picture:

Drag the Text toolbar out of the way if it covers the Menu bar, or the start point for the text box.

Select the Text tool and create a box to hold the text. If you get a message saying there's not enough room to paste text, enlarge the text box and try again.

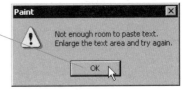

Select Edit, Paste to transfer the text. You can reposition parts of the text, insert tabs and change the font size or style.

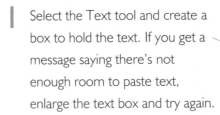

When it is entered as text, the data loses its formatting. Only one font can be used and any changes will apply to the whole selection.

Click outside the text box to end.

Cut and paste images

1 Open Paint and load the bitmap image you want to copy. Click the Select tool and mark the area of the image that you want to copy.

Use the Free-Form Select tool for irregular shapes.

The process for moving image data through the Clipboard is similar to that for text.

2 Click Edit, Copy to transfer the image data to the Clipboard.

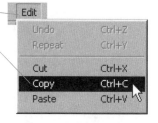

The contents of the Clipboard may be squeezed or stretched to fill the Viewer window.

The default format is Picture (Metafile). To see the image as it will look when pasted into a document, select View, Bitmap.

3 Run the ClipBook Viewer (see page 128) to display the contents of the Clipboard in the default format.

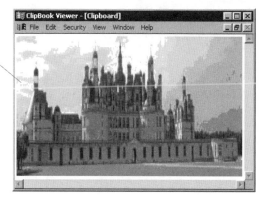

Add images to text

You can add an image to a text document as long as the application supports both types of data.

1 Load WordPad and open the target document that is to receive the image from the Clipboard.

2 Position the cursor at the point where the image should be inserted, adding a blank line if necessary.

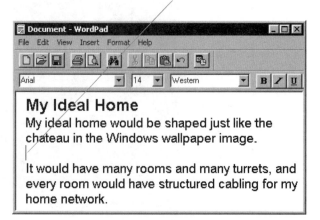

3 Click the Paste button (or select Edit, Paste) to add the image to the document. It will be inserted as a bitmap in its proper perspective, and at the chosen position.

The image will be shown in the correct size and proportion, despite the stretching that may have been shown by the ClipBook viewer.

4 Right-click the image and select Bitmap Image Object, Edit. The Paint tools and menus replace the WordPad items, and the colour palette is displayed.

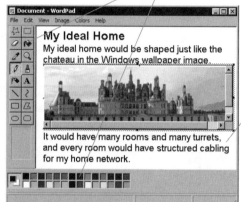

WordPad has the Paint toolbox and palette, so you can edit the inserted bitmap.

5 Click outside the image area to remove the Paint elements and return to the normal WordPad setup.

6 If you select Bitmap Image Object, Open instead of Edit, Paint will open in a separate window. Then you can modify the image and save it back into the document or as a separate file.

Double-click the icon to view or change the image in Paint.

7 To hide the image away until it is specifically requested, right-click the image and select Object Properties. Click the View tab and choose Display as Icon. Click OK, and an icon will replace the image.

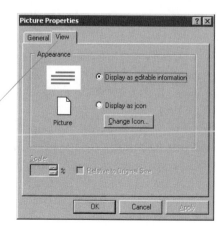

Paste to Notepad

To copy text information from the Clipboard:

Notepad supports plain text only and does not allow graphics, so the options for pasting objects will be constrained.

1 With text in the Clipboard, start Notepad and select Edit. Click Paste to insert the Clipboard contents.

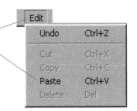

2 The data is inserted as plain text, with no formatting, using the current default font.

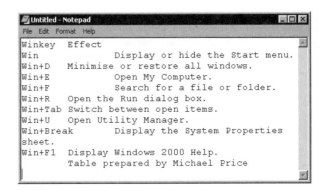

You can edit the data and change the font type or style, but format changes apply not only to the whole insert but to the whole document.

When you have an image rather than text data in the Clipboard, you'll find that Notepad is unable to handle it.

3 With an image in the Clipboard, select Edit in Notepad. You'll see the Paste function greyed (disabled), since there is no data that Notepad is designed to handle.

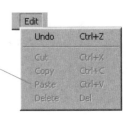

Word and the other Office applications also have their own Clipboard which can hold up to 24 items.

At the other end of the spectrum, you will find word processing applications with extra Paste options to match their additional capabilities, e.g. the Word Paste as Hyperlink option.

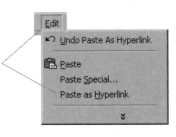

Cut and Paste

There are several ways to specify the actions you want when you are transferring information to and from the Clipboard:

Action	Keyboard	Menu bar	
Move to Clipboard	Ctrl+X	Edit, Cut	✂
Copy to Clipboard	Ctrl+C	Edit, Copy	🗐
Copy from Clipboard	Ctrl+V	Edit, Paste	📋
Undo last action	Ctrl+Z	Edit, Undo	↶

Graphics programs like Paint provide selection tools to help you mark the section of image to transfer. For text programs like WordPad, you can use the mouse to mark out the selection. To specify an area of text:

I Move the mouse pointer to the start of the data, press and hold the left button.

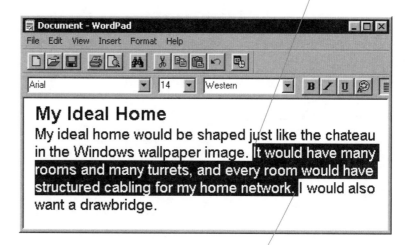

2 Drag the pointer to the end point and release.

It is often more precise to select text with the keyboard. For example, to mark an area of text, move the cursor to the start point, press and hold the Shift key then move the cursor using the arrow keys to highlight the required data. Finally, release the Shift key.

Drag-and-Drop

You do not always need the Clipboard to copy or move data between applications. You can use the drag-and-drop method.

This differs from the Clipboard method since the data does not get saved and cannot be used for repeat copies. There are also limitations, since not all applications support the process. WordPad does, but Paint and Notepad do not. To copy information with drag-and-drop, follow these steps:

1 Run WordPad and open the source document with the text to be copied.

2 Load a second copy of WordPad and open the target document.

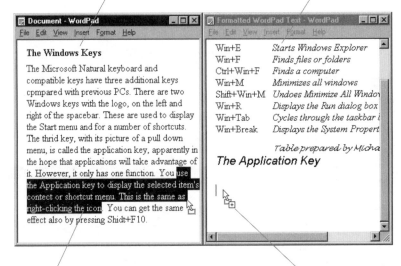

As the selection moves over areas where text cannot be inserted, a No Entry symbol is displayed:

3 Highlight the text you want to copy.

4 Click and drag to move the selection.

Hold down Ctrl before releasing the button, if you want to Copy a selection into the same document.

5 Position the text in the target location in the document, using the vertical bar to see where the text appears. Release the mouse button and the copy completes.

The mouse pointer changes as you drag and, as you cross over to the other document, a plus sign [+] is added. This indicates Copy, rather than Move, which is the default when you Drag a selection within the same document.

Clip from Command Prompt

You can copy text from a Command Prompt window.

1. In the Command Prompt window, right-click the Title bar to display the menu, and click Edit and then Mark.

2. Click the beginning of the text to be copied. Press and hold the Shift key, and click the end of the text. Right-click the Title bar, click Edit and then Copy.

You cannot paste text into a Command Prompt window or MS-DOS-based program when it is running in a full screen.

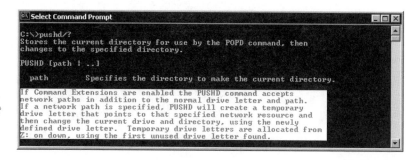

3. To paste the text, position the cursor and select Edit, Paste from the Title bar menu or the Windows program Menu bar.

In some MS-DOS-based programs, QuickEdit mode is not available.

4. To copy and paste MS-DOS text using the mouse (without needing Edit, Mark), select Properties from the menu, select the QuickEdit Mode option and click OK.

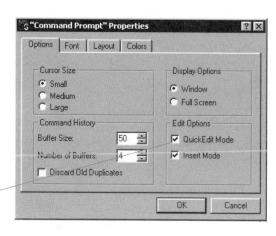

Embedded objects

You are using OLE when you cut and paste, but Windows takes care of the mechanics for you.

When you use the Copy and Paste functions to add data from one application into a document created by another dissimilar application, you are building a compound document with embedded objects. Windows uses Object Linking and Embedding (OLE) to manage these compound documents. The application that creates the enveloping document is known as the container or client. The application that supplies and edits the object is referred to as the server, because it supplies OLE services to the client.

When changes are needed, instead of having to edit the data in the originating application and repeating the copy and paste, you can edit the data in situ, without having to exit the client. You just double-click the object and the menus and toolbars change from their normal settings to provide the functions of the server. When you finish making changes, click outside the object area to restore the original client application menus and toolbars.

You can embed information using the copy and paste commands, or by using drag-and-drop if the application supports it. However, if the object is the whole file, rather than a section of the file, there is another method available. You can Insert the object file, and either embed it or link it in the document. To illustrate:

In this example, one user creates an item (a logo), the second reviews the work and the third has authority to make alterations.

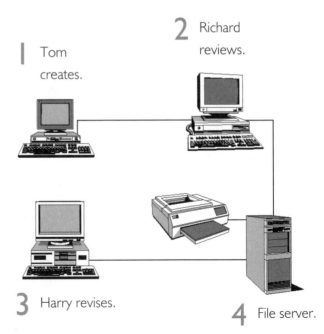

2 Richard reviews.

1 Tom creates.

3 Harry revises.

4 File server.

...cont'd

Use OLE to include an image file in a document and share it over the LAN.

| When the logo has been created and is ready, set up a document to contain the image and associated notes.

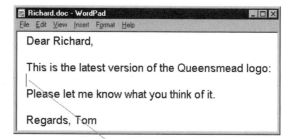

2 Position the cursor at the location for the image and click Insert, Object.

Click the Browse button to search for the file, if you don't know the full path.

3 Click Create from File, type the file name and click OK.

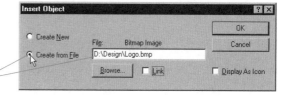

Similarly, any changes the user may make to the document image are not reflected in the original file.

The embedded object is a one-way, one-time transfer of data between the applications.

The image object is inserted into the document. Users with access to this document see the image exactly as it appears in the original file. However, any subsequent changes to that image file will not be reflected in the document image.

Linking objects

When you link data, details of the source file are retained in the document.

The embedded data is stored in the document, even with Icon view.

The OLE details are used to identify the source application and original file for edit purposes.

If changes are allowed, or if the document must be kept up-to-date, the file should be linked rather than embedded.

To link a file object into a WordPad document:

1 Open the document, position the typing cursor and click Insert, Object.

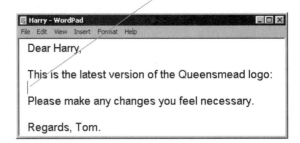

2 Click Create from File, type the file name, click the Link box and click OK.

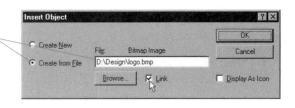

Changes made are reflected in all documents with links to the image file.

Linked objects form a two-way dynamic data exchange.

The object is inserted into the document. The user again sees the image as it appears in the original. However, when the image is double-clicked, it opens a separate window for the Paint program with the original image file. Any changes that are made will be saved directly to the original.

You can check to see if there are any links defined in the open document.

3 Select Edit from the Menu bar and click Links to view and modify the links in the document. (If Links is greyed, there are none defined.)

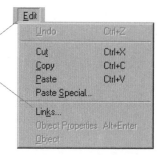

If you change the name or path of the source document or server application, you must re-establish your links.

4 Select an entry and click Update Now to refresh the copy that is stored in the document.

5 Click Open Source to view or change the original file.

6 You may find other types of links including music or video files.

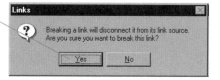

7 Click Change Source to specify a different path or file name for the selected source file, when the link is marked Unavailable.

8 Make updates automatic for the selected link (by selecting Automatic) to get the copy refreshed when you open the document.

The copy remains in the document, but the item is dropped from the Links list.

9 Click Break Link then Yes if you no longer want updates when the source document is altered.

OLE Registration

You can set up a link between two separate applications or documents only when both support OLE.

As well as handling Paint images and MIDI files, WordPad can insert data objects and files from any application that supports OLE, including Office applications such as Excel and PowerPoint and the Office mini applications such as Equation and WordArt.

To check what OLE-compatible applications and objects are currently registered on your system:

1 Open the System Information utility from the Systems Tools folder in the Start menu.

2 Click the [+] to expand Software Environment (it changes to [-]), and then select the OLE Registration branch.

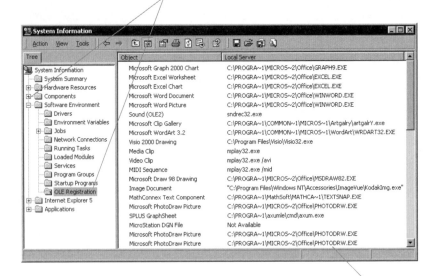

The example shown has Windows 2000 components, plus objects from Office, Visio and other applications.

3 A message "Refreshing system information" appears, and after a moment the list of objects is displayed, along with the relevant application program name.

If you have Windows 2000 alone installed, you may have very few entries, but each OLE compliant application that you install will add one or more entries to the list.

Controlling the Printer

This chapter looks at the Printers folder, and shows you how to add local and network printers; print from applications or via shortcuts; and manage print queues and paper changes.

Covers

Windows printers | 146

Adding printers | 147

Manual install | 148

Printer properties | 150

Network printers | 152

Driver verification | 154

Application printing | 155

Creating a print queue | 156

Document printing | 158

Generic text printers | 160

Print and hold | 162

Many printers in one | 163

Replacing printers | 164

Chapter Eight

Windows printers

Windows 2000 records information about its printers in the special Printers folder. You can access this from the Control Panel or from the Settings folder:

1 Double-click the Printers icon in the Control Panel, or select Start, Settings, Printers.

Printers

You can add extra definitions that represent different uses of the same printer to save you having to change the properties.

2 The Printers folder opens to show the Add Printer wizard and defined printers, if any.

The default Windows 2000 installation will have no printers defined unless Windows was able to recognise and define them during Setup. With a pre-installed system your supplier may have added printer definitions for you. There may be a definition for a fax printer, used to send documents as faxes, if you have a fax modem installed. There may also be definitions for printers attached to other PCs on your network.

If you changed settings for the Start menu to expand the Printers folder, it will display the wizards and printer definitions in a menu list. Double-click the Printers entry to open the folder instead.

Adding printers

The printer wizard guides you through the steps for defining a printer.

1 Open the Printers folder and double-click Add Printer. When the wizard starts, click Next.

Select Network printer if the printer is on the network, or if you are planning to create files to send to another PC for printing.

2 Select Local or Network printer. For a Local Printer, you can ask Windows to automatically detect and install a Plug-and-Play printer.

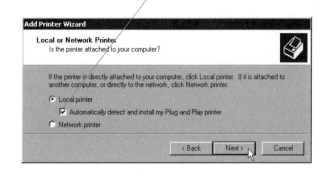

Most printers can identify themselves to Windows on request, so installation can be automated, unless you have an older printer.

If the printer is not Plug-and-Play, or if you've switched off detection, you can install the printer manually (see page 148).

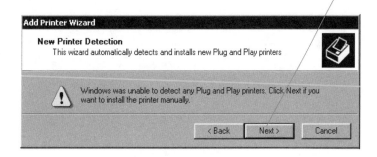

Manual install

1 Select the port address. This is usually LPT1. Then select the manufacturer and the model from the list provided.

Type the initial letter of the maker's name to position yourself at the right part of the list.

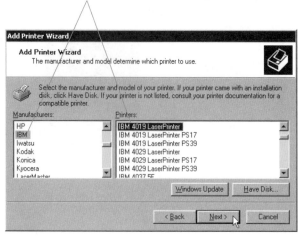

You may use the device CD, or you could find a copy of the device driver on the Internet at the manufacturer's site.

Windows 2000 includes drivers for a large number of printers. If your printer does not appear to be among them, click the Have Disk button and insert the device disk for your printer. Select your model of printer from the list provided.

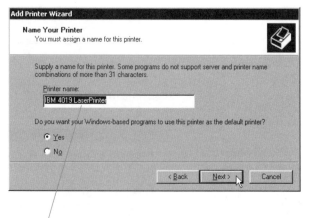

2 Specify a name for the printer, and indicate if it will be shared. For a printer that may be used on a network, you can put a description and location details.

...cont'd

3 Click Finish to close the wizard.

The wizard summarises all the selections you have made. Click Back if you need to make any changes.

Windows installs and configures the printer. Be ready to insert the Windows 2000 Setup CD if requested. The printer driver software and any other files required will be copied onto your hard disk.

An icon for the printer is added to the Printers folder and, assuming this is the first printer installed on your PC, it is made the default

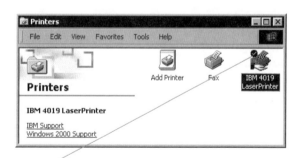

printer, as shown by the tick on the printer icon.

It is best to request a test page, to make sure that everything is working the way you expect.

If requested, a test page will be generated, and will show the printer driver names, version numbers and dates, so you can check you have the latest level.

Printer properties

The printer properties define in detail the functions and operations available for that printer. There are several ways to display the Properties page for a printer:

1 Open the Printers folder, and right-click the printer to display the context menu.

The tick moves from the original printer to the selected printer, which now becomes the default.

2 If the printer is not already the default, click here to set it.

3 You can manage the printer from this menu, setting paper preferences, pausing the print job and setting sharing options.

The Properties pages that are displayed will be specific to the printer type, so each printer may have a different set of tabs and options available.

4 Click Properties and select the Device Settings tab to check that device characteristics are correct. Specify paper sizes and

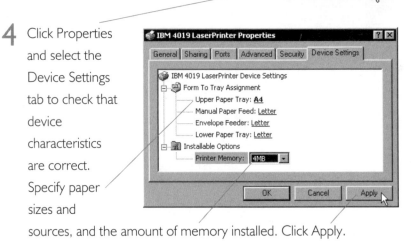

sources, and the amount of memory installed. Click Apply.

5 Select the Security tab to choose which groups can control the printer and the print queues.

...cont'd

6 Select the Advanced tab to make changes to the way the printer operates.

You can have several definitions for the same printer, each with different settings.

Set the priority (1 lowest, 99 highest).

Specify if printing is to start immediately or after transfer.

Hold mismatched documents in the queue. This will not stop other jobs from printing.

Specify when the printer will be available.

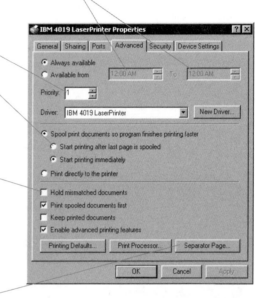

There is a mismatch when the printer and document setups do not match e.g. each might be set to use a different paper size.

Specify a separator page. This is useful if the printer is shared.

7 Select the General tab to check the description and features, set your paper preferences and request a test page.

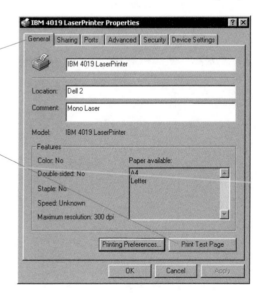

Network printers

If your PC is connected to a network, you may be able to share a printer attached to a server or another PC. Before you can use the printer, however, you will have to define the printers involved for your copy of Windows.

Before starting, confirm with the PC owner or with your network administrator that the printer is set up for sharing over the network, and that your user ID has been assigned authority to access it. You will also require:

*   The printer name and the server or PC name.

*   The manufacturer and the model for the printer.

1 Open the Printers folder, double-click Add Printer, and click Next. Select Network Printer and then click Next.

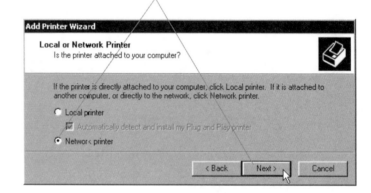

Another way to add a network printer is to open My Network Places and browse the PCs shown. When you find a printer to attach, right-click it and select Install. This will open Add Printer but you will be several steps further forward.

2 Specify the network address for the printer, using the UNC (Universal Naming Convention) path e.g. \\R400\QMS.

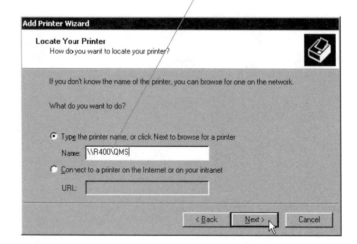

...cont'd

*If you are not sure of the address, leave the name blank and click **Next** to browse the PCs on the network that have shared printers.*

3 Select the printer from the list of printers available on your network. Click the [+] to expand the list for a PC.

You must connect to the LAN before adding the printer, so that Windows can locate the drivers needed.

If the printer is on a Windows 2000 PC, the required driver will be transferred and the printer will be ready to use. If it's a different operating system, or if the network is not currently up, you'll be asked for the location of the driver.

If the printer is on a Windows 2000 PC, you can specify drivers for any other operating system that may need to connect to it.

4 Select the maker and model from the list, or click Have Disk, insert the device disk and browse to the driver folder.

Driver verification

The Systems Information tool contains the File Signature Verification program that checks the files on your system.

The system files supplied on the Windows 2000 CD have a digital signature to confirm they are original, unaltered files. If you use a device disk from the manufacturer, especially if it contains an older device driver such as the Windows NT 4 version, you may be warned that the file is unsigned.

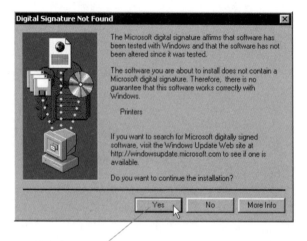

When more new versions of device drivers are issued, with specific support for Windows 2000, this problem will arise less often.

1 If the disk is from a trusted source, and you know it works with Windows 2000, click Yes to continue.

When the wizard completes, the new printer will be added to the folder.

2 Open the Printers folder to check the printers.

3 Click a printer icon to get information about its location and status.

4 Right-click the icon to change its Properties.

Application printing

The printer properties will be adopted for the application, but you can change some parts of the printer configuration from within the application itself. When the job is sent to the printer, you can carry on with other tasks, because Windows 2000 has a print spooler that handles the work in the background.

To print from an application such as WordPad:

1 Print the current document by clicking the Print button on the toolbar. This sends the job to the default printer, without giving you an opportunity to change settings.

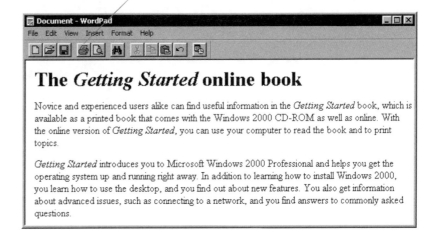

2 Select File from the Menu bar and select Print Preview to see how the output will appear.

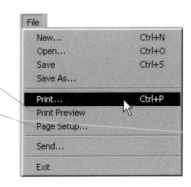

3 Select Page Setup to change the paper size or margins.

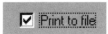
4 Select Print to choose the printer and to change its properties.

Creating a print queue

The properties set in the document must match the properties set for the printer definition. If you are using a network printer, the definitions on your PC and on the PC with the printer actually attached must also match.

Check in particular that you set the paper size in each, since the default is often Letter rather than A4.

Selecting File, Print displays a window that allows you to change settings for that print job. The window shows the current printer name and status. You can:

Click the Layout or the Paper/Quality tab to change the Properties.

Change to a different printer.

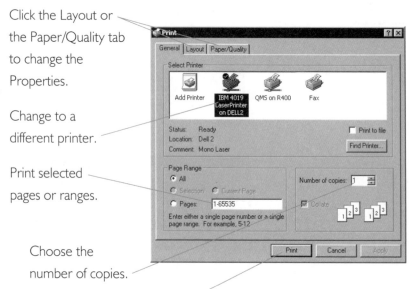

Print selected pages or ranges.

Choose the number of copies.

| Select Print to start generating printer data from the document.

The application does not print the document directly, it just transfers the printer-ready data to the Windows print spooler.

When printing begins, an icon is added to the System tray, showing that the Windows print spooler is active, and providing a quick point of access to the printer management functions.

2 Right-click the Printer icon in the System tray to show the active printers.

...cont'd

The print spooler runs in the background and handles the printer and print requests from other applications on the PC and (if it is a networked printer) across the network.

You wait only until the document has been prepared and transferred to the spooler, then you can carry on working on a different document, or quit the application and start another.

The application can have more than one job outstanding, and several applications may be using the printer at the same time. This means that a queue of print jobs can build up. The data files for the jobs are stored on the hard disk while they wait their turn.

To view the status of the printers:

1 Double-click the printer icon in the System tray, and the printer spoolers for all the active printers are started.

This shows the print spoolers on the application PC. There will also be print spoolers running on the printer server PC. These will show similar information, and you can manage jobs from either PC, if you have the required authorisation level.

You cannot pause or cancel jobs from other users, unless you have administrator privileges on the printer.

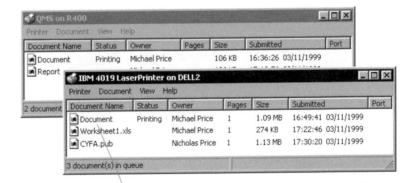

2 Right-click the print job, and select Pause to prevent it being printed when its turn arrives, or to stop further data being sent for that job.

3 Right-click the print job, and select Resume to reactivate the job, Restart to print from the beginning or Cancel to remove the job from the queue.

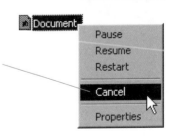

Document printing

You'll need access to the printer icon. You can use the icons in the Printers folder, but it is easier if you create a printer shortcut on the Desktop:

Open the Printers folder, right-click the printer and select Create Shortcut. Click Yes to create the shortcut on your Desktop.

To print using drag-and-drop:

Locate the document icon, drag it to the printer icon and drop it when the icon changes colour.

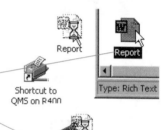

2 The appropriate application (for example, Word with a .DOC file) starts up, formats the document and sends it to the spooler for the selected printer. Finally, it closes itself down.

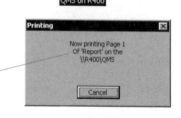

To print using the context menu:

Right-click the document icon and select Print from the context menu.

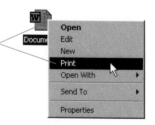

The application is loaded as before. Note that if the application is already running, Windows uses that copy to process the document.

...cont'd

To print to your choice of printer using the context menu, add printer shortcuts to the SendTo folder.

There is a SendTo folder for each user name defined on the system, but none in the All Users or Default User folders.

2 Create shortcuts on the Desktop to all the printers that you may need to use.

3 Open Windows Explorer, Documents and Settings and select a specific User name. Select Tools, Folder Options to Show hidden files and select the SendTo folder.

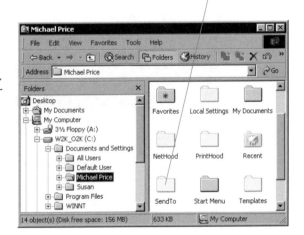

4 Drag-and-drop the shortcuts into the Send To folder.

This will start the application to send the document to the chosen printer.

5 Right-click the document and select Send To followed by your printer of choice.

Generic text printers

Printer control codes and control sequences initiate specific actions on the printer, and are used when the device driver does not support special features of the printer.

You can define a generic text printer to send control information to a printer. You enter the codes in a plain text file, obtaining the control sequences from the printer documentation.

You can install a generic text printer from the Printers folder, to process the file.

1 Run the Add Printer wizard to define a local printer.

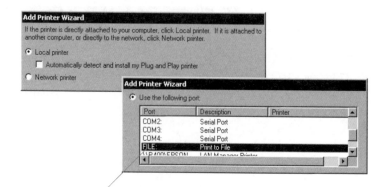

To save time, do not let the wizard search for plug-and-play devices.

2 Choose to use the File port, to send the data directly to a text file. Choose maker Generic and model Generic/Text Only.

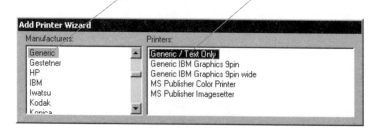

Select No to the options to make it the Windows default or to make it shareable.
Set the Properties to use continuous paper, with no page breaks, to avoid having headers interspersed in the output.

3 The text printer is added to the folder. Right-click the icon and select Preferences to set the printer properties.

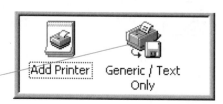

...cont'd

Click Show to display headings and select a heading, to have the option to print subtopics as well.

To capture the text from a Help file page using the generic text printer:

1 Click Options and select Print. Choose to print the selected topic.

This text printer may be handy to convert documents into a form suitable for plain text email, or to capture text from an application that has no save-to-file option.

2 Choose the generic text printer.

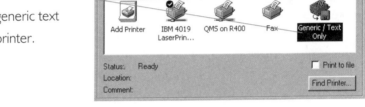

Help will generate a temporary HTML file containing the information, and ask you for the file name for the printed data.

3 Specify the file name. It is best to include the path, and you can add a file type (.PRN) if you wish.

Note that the output will contain line breaks and a left hand margin. You can edit the file using Notepad or WordPad and adjust the layout or add control sequences.

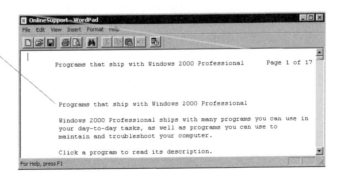

Print and hold

With a mobile PC or a network printer, you may not always have the printer available when you're ready to print. In Windows 2000 you can send documents to the printer but put the printing on hold until it is connected. This uses the offline printing feature.

To use offline printing:

1 Open the Printers folder, right-click the printer and choose Use Printer Offline.

 Offline printing is not used with network printers, so for these you must use the Pause option instead.

2 The printer icon is greyed to show that it is now offline. The print jobs created from now on will be held in the print queue until you wish to print.

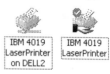

 When you are disconnected from the network, you can print to local printers, but you cannot print to shared printers on the network. Instead, the file is spooled and prints to your local printer when you are reconnected to the network.

3 Choose Printer from the Menu bar and deselect Use Printer Offline.

You must be using Windows spooling, so this method may not work with printers that provide their own spooling programs. However these usually have a Pause or Hold feature that can be used instead.

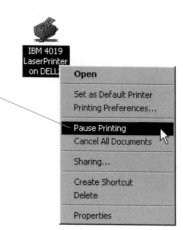

Another way to handle offline printing is to change the printer port to File, and create a print file that you can print directly when you are next online, using a printer definition that accepts RAW (printer-ready) data.

Many printers in one

Your printer may offer several different modes of operation that need different settings in the Properties.

At times, you may want to print in draft mode; at others, high-resolution graphics printing may be the order of the day. Then again, you may want to switch between Landscape and Portrait orientation, or you may have several different paper sources to suit particular types of jobs... You can, of course, change properties between every print job, but a far more effective way is to set up each configuration that you want as a separate printer definition.

To add a new definition:

1 Open the Printers folder, start the Add Printer wizard and reinstall your printer.

You must repeat the whole process for each different setup that you require: Landscape, Portrait, Draft, Graphics etc.

2 Choose to keep the existing device drivers for the printer.

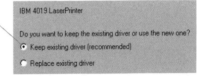

3 Change the name, choosing one related to the proposed use of the printer, and change the printer properties to suit.

Match the definitions to actual printer setups e.g. if you choose a printer definition with a different type of paper in the paper tray, make sure that the actual paper in the physical printer has been changed also.

4 Choose the printer definition to match your printing requirements of the moment.

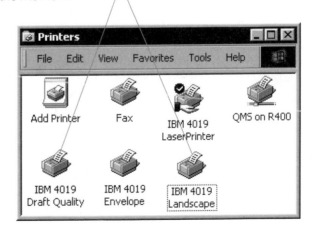

Replacing printers

You can delete a local or a network printer from the Printers folder.

If you change printer models, you can add the new printer. You can make it the new default printer when you install the printer driver, or by changing the printer properties (see page 150). You can leave the old printer icon in the folder, in case you need to revert to your old printer later.

If you'd prefer to remove unnecessary entries:

1 Open the Printers folder and right-click the icon for the redundant printer.

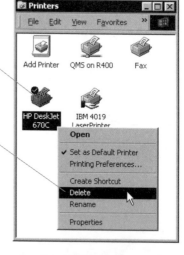

If the printer that you are deleting is currently the default, an alternative will be selected.

2 Select Delete from the menu and click Yes to confirm the removal.

The wizard selects the first printer in the folder as the default. If the one chosen is not suitable, right-click another printer and make it the new default printer.

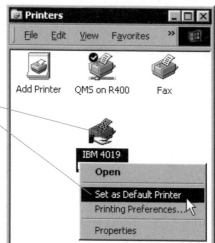

The driver for the deleted printer is retained on the hard disk, so you will be able to add that printer without the Windows 2000 CD-ROM or other printer device disk.

Note that some printers have their own management software, and for these you may need to run their Uninstall program to remove Start menu entries.

Networking Windows 2000

This chapter introduces networks (with the emphasis on designing, installing and using a workgroup) and peer-to-peer networking using the features supplied in Windows 2000. Finally, it examines the use of Windows Update to help keep the system up to date.

Covers

PC networks | 166

Server-based LANs | 168

Peer-to-peer LANs | 169

Planning the network structure | 170

Getting help with the design | 172

Higher speeds | 174

Adapter cards | 175

Network setup | 176

Sharing devices | 178

Browsing the network | 180

Mapping drives and folders | 182

Connecting two PCs | 184

Windows Update | 185

Chapter Nine

PC networks

This introduces networks for the small office or home environment, as it evolves from the stand-alone PC.

If you have more than one PC in your office, you may find yourself wanting to use the devices attached to one PC while working at another PC. For example, you may have specific devices such as a laser printer and a scanner attached to a particular PC.

The items that you can share include internal devices and adapters such as disk drives and modems.

The other PC may have devices of its own that it can share, or it may be a desktop or laptop PC without any attached peripherals. It could be an older machine that lacks features such as a CD-ROM drive, and may not even be running Windows 2000.

In any of these cases, you may wish for a method of linking your PCs together so that they can share each other's equipment.

This is exactly what a PC network achieves, but the implications go beyond merely sharing hardware. Because the PCs can access the drives on another PC, they can share data as well as devices.

This makes it possible to maintain consistent information on connected PCs, either by sharing one working copy, or by providing automatic updating when changes are made. This avoids the risk of data files being changed unilaterally and providing conflicting answers.

...cont'd

A network that spreads across separate locations is known as a Wide Area Network or WAN.

The connections between the PCs could be created in various ways, depending on their locations and on the type of data sharing you need. For example:

- PC to PC via a modem and telephone line.

- With email and file transfer services.

- Using the Internet and shared Web space.

- Direct connections using cables and adapter cards.

When you connect two or more PCs together in the same physical location, you create a Local Area Network, or LAN. The connections for the network require both hardware and software components.

The hardware provides the physical path between the PCs and includes:

For some types of network adapter, no hub device will be required.

- Adapter cards, one per PC, (or equivalent mother board connections).

- One (or more) central switch or hub.

- Network cables to connect the PCs to the hubs.

All of the necessary components may be found in Windows 2000 Professional, though for some types of network you may choose to use additional specialised software, to increase security or manage larger numbers of PCs.

Software is required to allow the PCs to communicate across the cables and adapters, and may include:

- Network client software for each PC.

- A network operating system for the controlling PC server (if one is used).

- Network transport protocols (the language rules for communicating over the network).

Network rules are needed to ensure that the data transfers between PCs are completed, and any errors that may arise are detected and corrected.

Server-based LANs

Networks started out in the corporate environment, where central control is often demanded.

There are two main ways of organising Local Area Networks. The most powerful and flexible approach is to place all the shared resources onto dedicated machines which are known as servers.

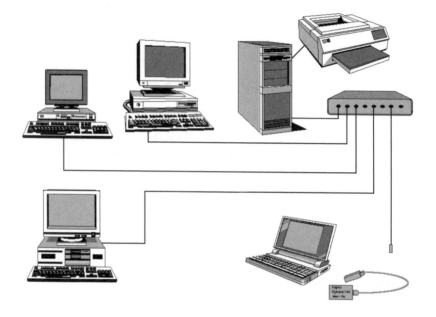

The servers could be PCs or larger computers, running a special-purpose network operating system such as Windows 2000 Server Novell Netware. The servers also manage the access facilities permitted for individual users and PCs connected to the network. The PCs may run any operating system that supports the client software needed to communicate with the server system. Windows 2000 contains the software needed to communicate with most network systems.

This is a lot of effort when all you want is to connect three or four PCs, so a simpler way has been developed.

Because of the complexity involved and to preserve the security of the system, the server networks usually require a network administrator whose job includes defining new workstations and new users to the system, and managing required changes to access levels and resource allocations.

In a smaller office or home environment, where there is only a small number of PCs, and the security requirements are less rigorous, a simpler network is more appropriate.

Peer-to-peer LANs

This method allows you to share devices without having to give them up to a central support unit.

The peer-to-peer network provides independence by allowing any PC to act as a server. The resource to be shared remains on the original PC, but the PC concerned provides access for other PCs on the network to files, folders, disk drives, printers, fax modems, scanners or CD-ROM drives. Every PC in the network can also function as a client to access resources on the other PCs in the network. The peer-to-peer network PCs share resources without demanding centralised control or administration, since each user in the network acts as the network administrator to assign shared resources and levels of access.

Windows 2000 has all the software to support a peer-to-peer network, for server and client aspects, without calling for a high level of technical expertise.

By the same token, the security it gives is more limited and may be viewed as a form of voluntary self-protection, to stop accidental loss of data, rather than to ensure complete privacy.

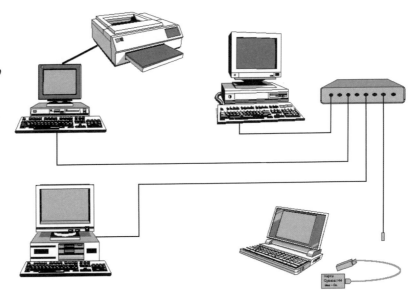

You can start off with a peer-to-peer network, and move towards a server-based network by dedicating some PCs to manage shared resources. Later you could upgrade these PCs with Windows 2000 Server software and make them into true servers. At the same time, you would be advised to lock the PCs in a server cabinet or room, to add the physical security needed to complement the increased access control that they can provide. You will also want to assign the task of network administration for the new server-based network to a trained technician.

Planning the network structure

The effort you should spend in planning your network will depend on the number of PCs that will be connected and the number of users that will share access to those PCs. However, for a small or a large network, you'll need to investigate the purpose and requirements, including:

- The resources that need to be shared (files, printers, modems, scanners).

- The volumes of data that may be involved (including printer files, scanner images etc.).

- The number of connections, now and in the future.

- The size in terms of separation between the PCs.

- The software used on the PCs. Older PCs for example may still be running Windows 3.x or MS-DOS.

- The level of security and control that you want.

The specification of these will determine the type of network connection you should choose, and whether you'll need a peer-to-peer network or a server-based network.

Bus topology

The simplest way to connect your PCs is using the bus topology where each PC is connected by coaxial cable using a T-piece connector, with terminators at each end. This supports up to 30 PCs, for a total length of 185 metres.

This is suitable for small numbers of PCs connected over a limited area, and is easy to set up and to extend, within the constraints noted. There's no problem running the network with some PCs powered off. However, a faulty cable or connector can cause the whole network to fail.

Star topology

Connecting PCs in a star topology requires a cable from each PC to a central connection device known as a hub.

In the star network, PCs are linked to a central point, like spokes on a wheel!

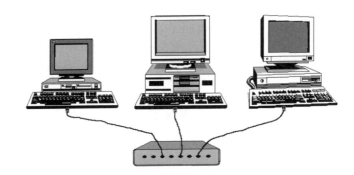

Hubs can be chosen to handle various numbers of PCs, for example 8, 16 or 24. The cable used is twisted-pair wire rather than coaxial, which is similar to telephone wire, and uses four pairs of wires and RJ-45 connectors that are also similar to some types of telephone connectors. The limit with the star network is that the maximum distance from hub to PC is 100 meters from the hub. This supports network speeds up to 10 Mbps, unless you choose the higher specification category 5 cable, which supports up to 100 Mbps.

With the star network, a defective cable affects only the one PC that it is connected to. On the other hand, the need to run all the cables to one point complicates the wiring. Also, the hub is a critical component. If it fails, the whole network fails.

There are wireless networks, which use infrared or radio links to eliminate the need for cabling – ideal if your business is located in a listed building.

Both problems are eased if you use multiple hubs and spread the PCs across them. However, the star network is more expensive than the bus network because of the cost of the hubs and because it requires more cable in total.

There are other types of cabling, including fibre optics, used to connect hubs at very high data rates, and there are many devices designed to extend the range of a LAN.

Getting help with the design

There's no shortage of help available to make it easier for you to design your network, whether you have a small or a large configuration in mind. Some companies specialise in the cabling aspects and will wire up your office, providing network access points for all your current and planned PCs. Other companies provide the hardware adapters, hubs and patch cables etc. that you need.

Call Black Box at 0118965 5000, or visit their website at: `http://www.blackbox.co.uk`

Black Box for example will provide a comprehensive catalogue with all the networking and communications hardware and supplies you could possibly want. The catalogue is a rich source of information, and there is also free technical support available, even if you are not a customer. You can describe your needs and receive suggested solutions that will meet your requirements.

This website is for information only, as is the technical support phone line, so you won't feel under pressure.
To buy products, you must call the dedicated sales lines.

For example, Black Box Technical Support were asked to provide a design for a network to connect seven users in a small office and to include potential for expansion in the future, They supplied a full range of answers, from the budget, cost-conscious solution, up to the no-holds-barred high speed setup, suitable for the most intensive networking applications.

...cont'd

The ballpark cost for a ThinNet setup would be £300 for eight users.

The bargain basement solution required seven ThinNet adapters, coax cabling, T-connectors and terminators, to provide a simple configuration which can be extended by simply adding more PCs with the appropriate adapters. This is the slowest network and the least robust.

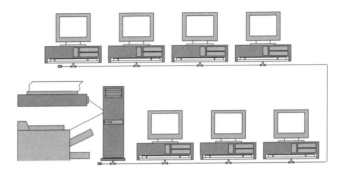

The budget 10 Base-T network would cost around £600 (all costs exclude cabling).

The budget solution included a 10 Mbps, 8-port hub, and 10 Mbps adapters for the PCs. The network can be extended by adding more hubs, but the speed will be limited to 10 Mbps unless all the components are replaced.

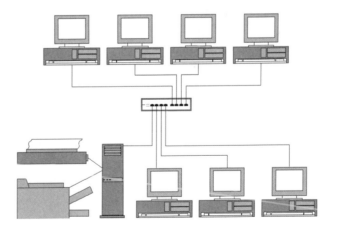

The ballpark cost is now £1500, to incorporate an enhanced network hub that can support a speed of 100 Mbps.

You can install dual speed 10/100 Mbps adapters and autodetect 10/100 Mbps hub. The PCs can then be operated at either 10 Mbps or 100 Mbps. This is worthwhile if you are working with large files, or sharing video or other multimedia data across the network.

Higher speeds

With more users and the higher data rate, the network becomes more susceptible to collisions between messages. That is, when two or more users transmit data at the same time, the messages interfere with each other, and it becomes necessary to pause and re-transmit, in the hope that the network has become clear.

The ballpark cost is £2200 for 100 Mbps, separate collision domains (excluding cabling).

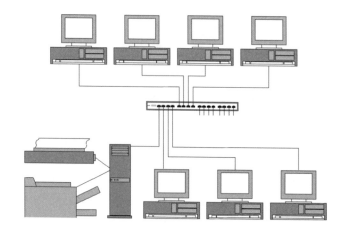

Pricing shown is for the main hardware components only. Actual costs will also depend on the cabling required.

If you replace the hub with an Ethernet Switch, then each user will be on their own 100 Mbps segment (separate collision domain). Any PCs with the slower 10 Mbps adapters will also be managed on separate segments. The server will be able to run at double speed, 200 Mbps full duplex, while the clients run at 100 Mbps duplex, and this will avoid a bottleneck at the server. This switch supports up to 12 users. Additional switches or hubs will be needed for further expansion.

Other solutions

This discussion has introduced just some of the issues involved in designing your network. There are many combinations of network components that you may want to consider, such as wireless configurations that use radio links instead of cable. As well as the network equipment itself, you need to investigate items concerned with housing the cables and servers; the hardware and software tools for monitoring and troubleshooting your network; and the training that will be required for the users of the network and for the people responsible for maintaining and updating your network configuration.

Adapter cards

When you have decided what type of cabling you will use, you can choose the type of network adapter card needed for each PC, to provide the interface to the network. You must check what type of adapter slots are available on your PCs. There are adapter cards suitable for PCI, ISA, EISA, Vesa local bus, Microchannel and PC Card (PCMCIA).

For the desktop PCs using the Pentium processor, the preferred choice is PCI, since these offer better performance and are easier to configure than the older ISA that was the previous standard.

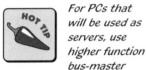
For PCs that will be used as servers, use higher function bus-master adapter cards which can handle data even when the main processor is busy.

There are two main varieties of card, distinguished by the type of connector:

1 Adapter with RJ-45 connector

2 Adapter with Coax T-connector

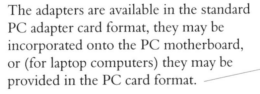

Choose an adapter with multiple connection types (a combo card) if you plan to start with a bus topology network but later switch to a star layout.

The adapters are available in the standard PC adapter card format, they may be incorporated onto the PC motherboard, or (for laptop computers) they may be provided in the PC card format.

If you have a separate network adapter, install it into your PC, following the guidelines provided in the documentation supplied with your PC or with the adapter card. When the adapters have been installed, connect the PCs to one another (for a bus topology network) or to the central hub (for a star topology network). Connect the hub to the power supply, and you are ready to configure your network.

The wizard may call for the Windows 2000 CD-ROM if all the network software is not already installed.

The following description is for a network adapter added to the PC after Windows 2000 has been installed. If you install or upgrade a PC with the network adapter already installed, the network connection will be automatically configured during setup, following a similar process.

Network setup

For adapters that are not plug-and-play, you can start the Add/ Remove Hardware wizard from the Control Panel to detect and install your network adapter card.

When the PC starts, Windows 2000 will detect the new hardware, if it is plug-and-play compatible, and will automatically start the Add/Remove Hardware wizard. Windows 2000 may include a suitable driver for the card, or you may insert the device diskette provided with the card to select the driver that it provides.

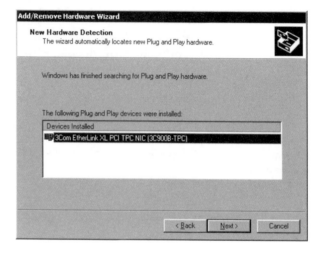

After the wizard completes, you can look in My Network Places to check the network related components that have been installed.

Open Network and Dial-up Connections in Control Panel, right-click Local Area Connection and select Properties.

...cont'd

All the requirements for Windows 2000 networking will be automatically selected and installed when the adapter is configured:

Windows 2000 enables the network adapter and configures the networking connection automatically.

Client for Microsoft Networks or Client for NetWare Networks

File and printer sharing

The Internet Protocol TCP/IP

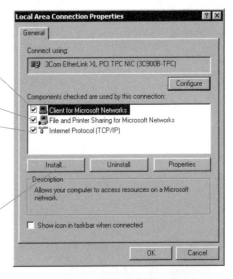

Click the box on the LAN Properties to show an icon in the System tray when the adapter is connected and the network is active.

If you want PCs still running Windows 98 to be part of the network, you will need to add the NetBEUI protocol.

2 Click Install, select Protocol and click the Add button.

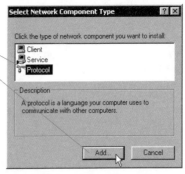

The NetBEUI protocol is added to the list in LAN Properties.

3 Select NetBEUI Protocol and click OK to add it. You will not need to restart the system.

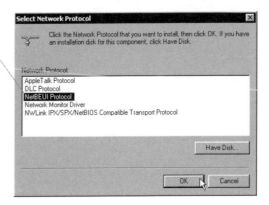

Sharing devices

Windows 2000 enables file and printer sharing when it configures the adapter, but you must explicitly define the drive, folder or printer that you are willing to share.

Before any other PC can share the devices on a networked PC, the PC owner must make the resources available. Note that to share devices, you must be logged on as an administrator or as a member of the power user group.

To share a device:

1. Open the folder containing the item you want to share e.g. open My Computer to share the D drive. Right-click the icon for the item and select Sharing.

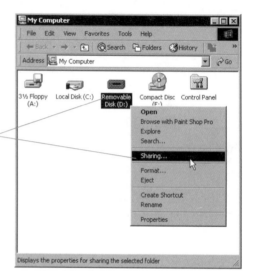

If you follow the name with a $ sign (e.g. C$) the folder will not be visible when users browse the network (see page 180) but they will be able to map to the folder or drive.

2. Select Share this folder. Provide a meaningful name for the device, and include the optional comment if desired.

3. The maximum number of concurrent users in Windows 2000 Professional is ten. To specify a lower limit, click Allow, then enter the number of users you will permit.

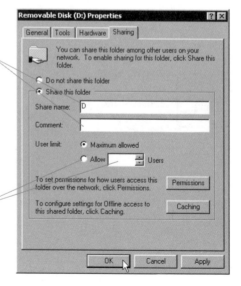

If a sharing option has already been defined for that drive, you can create another by clicking the New Share button.

...cont'd

4 Click the Permissions button earlier to specify the users and the type of access allowed. By default, all users with access to the network can read and write to the drive.

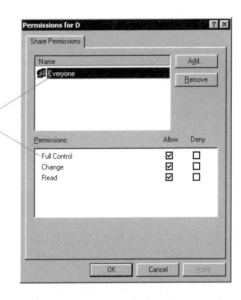

5 You can specify if caching is allowed for files within the shared folder. Click the Caching button earlier and select a caching type. Manual caching (file by file) is advised for documents.

6 The item's icon is updated with a server hand, to indicate sharing.

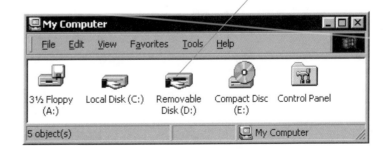

Browsing the network

You can see what resources other users have made available for sharing on the Local Area Network, through My Network Places (the updated version of Network Neighbourhood that includes dial-up as well as network connections).

You can display all the PCs, printers, files and folders on the network, or only those PCs and resources in your domain/ workgroup.

Double-click the My Network Places icon to browse resources across the entire network.

My Network Places

2 Double-click Computers Near Me to display the PCs in the domain or workgroup you specified during setup.

Windows searches for all the PCs that are part of your group and that are currently on line to the network.

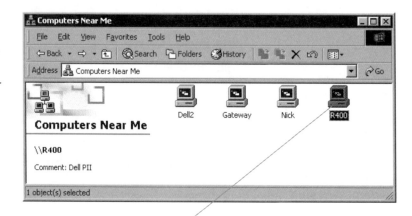

3 Double-click one of the PCs in the workgroup to see the items that it has made available for sharing.

...cont'd

You can explore the shared resources in any workgroup and in any PC on the network, except resources shared with a $ sign after the name to keep them private.

4 The files, folders and printers that have been shared will appear in the window:

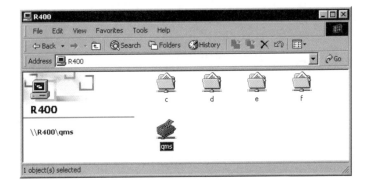

You cannot print to a network printer unless you are online – there is no printer caching, except for locally attached printers.

5 Before you can use a networked printer, the driver must be installed on your PC. It will be copied from the PC owning the printer.

6 You can open files directly from My Network Places in applications such as WordPad by clicking the Shortcut bar.

The Open dialog (as with other dialogs) has a Shortcut bar link to My Network Places.

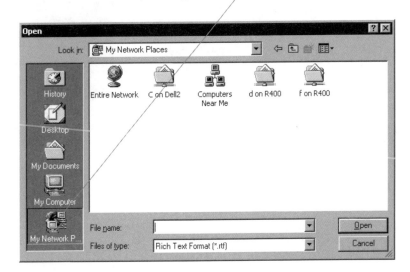

Mapping drives and folders

You can address networked folders and drives by their server names, or you can assign them a drive letter.

When you open a folder or drive from My Network Places, a shortcut to that item is added to the folder, so that it will be easy to reopen next time.

You can address files and folders by name, using the network address in place of the drive letter. For example, D:\Accounts on the D400 PC is addressed on other PCs as: \\D400\d\accounts.

To make such references easier, you can assign a drive letter to the shared item:

Another way is to locate the folder in My Network Places, right-click it and select Map Network Drive.

I Open Windows Explorer, select Tools from the Menu bar and click Map Network Drive.

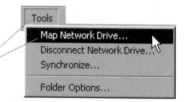

2 Accept the drive letter specified, or choose one from the list, and enter the server name for the folder or drive.

If you won't use this network folder often, clear the Reconnect at logon box. This will speed the Windows 2000 start-up.

3 Tick the box to map the device share at startup.

4 Click Browse if you are unsure of the correct server name, then follow step 5.

You will get *read-only* or *full access, as specified by the owner, or based* on the password you supply *if there are several options.*

5 Navigate through My Network Places (displayed in a tree format) to locate the folder or drive, and the server path is inserted into the appropriate field in the Map Drive window.

The new drive letter is added to the My Computer folder. It will appear every time you restart Windows, as long as the network is connected, if you chose the Reconnect at logon option.

If you want to work with some of the files when the network is disconnected, right-click the drive icon and select Make Available Offline.

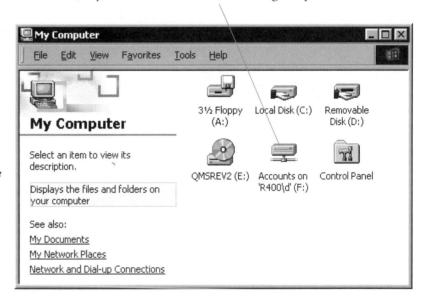

To discontinue mapping or to switch to a different drive letter:

Right-click the drive icon and select Disconnect.

Connecting two PCs

If there are only two PCs to connect, you do not need a full network setup.

The simplest network consists of two PCs connected to each other. This setup is commonly used in small offices or at home to share a printer or for exchanging files. It is also the setup for connecting a laptop PC to a desktop PC.

Crossover network cables are readily available, since they are the cables that are normally used for connecting the hubs in a larger network.

Cable connection

There are three connection methods that can be used:

- Coaxial cable and two bus network or combo adapters.

- Crossover twisted-pair cable and two star network adapters.

- Direct Cable Connection using a null modem or parallel port connection cable.

The direct cable connection is slower but uses the existing parallel or serial port. However, with DCC you can connect in to an existing LAN, accessing shared resources on the network from the laptop, through the network adapter of the connected PC.

Direct connections are useful for connecting devices such as palmtop computers to the network.

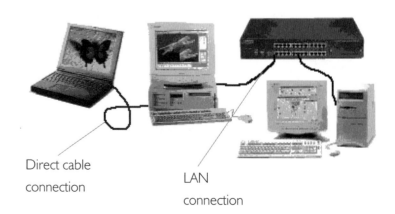

Direct cable connection

LAN connection

Windows Update

Windows Update will detect what fixes and functions are needed to bring your system right up-to-date and will download and install them for you.

1 Connect to the Internet and select Start, Windows Update. Internet Explorer starts up and displays the Windows Update home page.

2 Click the Product Updates link to obtain a list of updates.

If you have clicked in the box to indicate that Microsoft is a trusted supplier, you won't see the certificate or messages, unless the download file has been altered in any way.

3 Click Yes to install the Active Setup applet to your hard disk, so that it can identify the current status of your system. No data about your hardware or software will be sent to Microsoft.

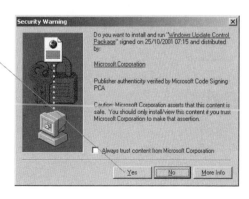

Note that updates are organised in the following groups:

- *Critical Updates*
- *Picks of the Month*
- *Recommended*
- *Additional Windows Features, and;*
- *Device Drivers*

4 Only items that apply to your version of Windows will be listed. Click Show Installed Updates to list all such items.

5 Select the updates that you wish to apply to your system and click the Download arrow.

6 The files are copied to your hard disk and then Setup is run automatically. You may have to restart the system to put the updates into effect.

When you connect to the Web, Windows Update can notify you when a new critical update (bug fix or security) becomes available.

Install the Critical Update Notification component from Product Updates to ensure that you keep your computer up-to-date. When a new Windows 2000 Professional update arrives at the site, you are notified the next time you connect to the Internet.

You can choose to update immediately, or defer the warning and visit the site to update at a convenient time.

Index

A

Accessibility
  Options 33
Accessories 55
Active Desktop 107, 109
Active Setup applet 185
Adapter cards 167, 175
Address bar 37
Administrator account 18
Applications
  Installing 49, 88–104
AutoRun 20, 90

B

Background printing 155
BIOS 12–13, 19
Black Box 172
Boot
  From CD-ROM 19
  From diskette 15, 19
  From network 19
Boot menu 24

C

Cabling 167, 170–172, 184
Calculator 33–34, 56

CD Player
  Download details 62
  Playlists 62
CD-ROM 15, 166, 169
CD-RW 37
Certified for Windows 88
Clients 8
Clipboard 126–127, 130–134, 136–138
ClipBook
  Viewing 128–129
Clock 37
Closing down 38
Cluster service 9
Command Prompt 57
Compatibility 88–89
Connect to the Internet 26
Context menu 42
Control Panel 29, 46–51, 53–54, 117, 176
  Options 46–47
Copy/Cut and Paste 41, 137
  Embedded objects 140–141
  Images 133–136
  OLE 144
Critical Update Notification 186
Cursor blink rate 53

D

Date/time 37, 50
Desktop
  Bar 37
  Default 106
  Content 27
  Customising 107–109
Device Manager 20
Dial-up status 78–79
Direct Cable Connection 184
Disk Operating System. *See* MS-DOS
Display properties 51
Document
  Term defined 126

Drag-and-Drop   30, 138, 140, 158–159
Driver verification   154
Dual-boot   14, 18

E

Email. *See* Internet mail
Entertainment   55, 62–65, 114

F

Favorites   30
Fax   43, 58
File
  Associations   44, 93
  Systems   16
Folder
  Options   44
  Views   40
Fonts
  Add new   52
  System display   112–113
  Viewing   52
Freecell   64
Frequency of program use   100

G

Games   64–65
Getting started
  Connect to the Internet   26
  Discover Windows   26
  Register Now   26
Graphical User Interface   17
Graphics
  Using MouseKeys for   47
GUI. *See* Graphical User Interface

H

Hardware
  Adding/removing   48
Hardware Compatibility List   13
HCL. *See* Hardware Compatibility List
Help   30

I

ICS. *See* Internet Connection Sharing
Infrared   43, 171
Initial tasks   26
Installing
  Applications   49, 88–104
    From zipped files   90, 97
    Managing the Start menu   104
    Migration   91
    Paint Shop Pro   92–93
    Preliminaries   88–89
    Reinstallation   89, 92
    Using Add/Remove   90, 94, 100–101
    Via Run   90, 96, 102
    Visio   94–95
    What to watch out for   98–99
  Windows 2000. *See* Windows 2000: Installing
Internet connection
  Connect to the Internet   68–69, 77
  Defining   68
  Dialup icon   77
  Disconnect   77
  Manual setup   71–72
  Modem   69
  Phone numbers   71, 78
  Protocols   78
  Proxy settings   73
  Retries   76
  Signon   77
  Via LAN   73
Internet Connection Sharing   8, 73, 82–83, 85
Internet Connection Wizard   68–69

Internet Explorer 27, 68, 80
  Clear history 80
  Connection to the Web 68
  Home page 81
  Open in same window 42
  Properties 80
  Temporary storage 80
Internet mail 74–75
Internet Service Providers 9, 68
  Choosing 70
  New account 26
  Referral
    List 69
    Server 69
  Registered 69
Iomega Zip disks 39
IP addressing 82, 84
ISP. *See* Internet Service Providers

K

Keyboard 17, 53, 124, 137
Kodak Imaging 58

L

LAN 12, 27, 49, 71, 73, 83–86, 153, 167–169,
    177, 180, 184
  Reconnect at logon 182
  Server-based 168
  Status 86
Layout
  Appearance 112–113
  Changing monitor frequency 116
  Colour 110
  Default Desktop 106–107
  Mouse settings 124
  Regional options 124
  Resolution 111
  Screensavers 114–115
  Start menu 118–119
  Taskbar 118–119

Tile wallpaper 108
Web content 109
Legacy applications 102
Local Area Network. *See* LAN
Locale 37
Logon/logoff 30

M

Mathcad 98
Media Player 62
Mice
  Acceleration 54
  Buttons
    Reversing 54
  Customising 124
  Double-click 54
  Motion 54
  Pointer response 54
  Single-click 54
MIDI. *See* Musical Instrument Device Interface
Minesweeper 64
Minimise windows 35
MouseKeys 47
Move or copy files 41
MS-DOS 57, 102
  Applications 103
Multimedia
  Preview 11
Musical Instrument Device Interface 144
My Computer 27, 40, 44, 46, 58, 66, 120
  Contents 28
  Drives 39
  Favorites 30
My Documents 27, 39, 43, 119
My Network Places 22, 27, 30, 39, 152, 176,
    180–183

N

Network Load Balancing   9
Networking   166–184
  Adapter cards   167, 175
  Black Box   172
  Browsing the network   180–181
  Bus topology   170
  Cabling   171, 184
  Client software   167
  Collision domain   174
  Computers Near Me   180
  Connection
    Cabling   170, 184
    Retaining settings   14
    Two PCs   184
  Connectors   175
  Dedicated servers   169
  Design help   172–173
  Disable   86
  Duplex operation   174
  Ethernet Switch   174
  Fibre optics   171
  Hub   167, 171
  Infrared or radio   171
  Mapping drives/folders   182–183
  My Network Places   22, 27, 30, 39, 152, 176, 180–183
  Offline files   183
  Operating system   167
  Peer-to-peer   8, 169
  Printer   152, 181
  Protocol   177
  Requirements   172, 177
  Setup   176–177
  Sharing data   166–167
  Sharing devices   166–167, 178–179
  SoHo   166
  Star topology   171
  Structure   170–171
NLB. *See* Network Load Balancing
Notepad   59
NTFS file system   16
Numeric keypad   56

O

Object Linking and Embedding. *See* OLE
OLE   125–126, 140–144
OLTP. *See* Online Transaction Processing
Online Transaction Processing   9
Open With   44
Outlook Express   37, 68, 74

P

Paint   60, 132, 142
Paint Shop Pro   92–93
Partition   14, 16
PartitionMagic   24
Paste Special   131
PC cards   175
PC-DOS. *See* MS-DOS
Peer-to-peer network   8, 169
Phone Book Administrator   96
Pinball   65
Plug-and-Play
  Network adapters   176
Print spooler   37, 155–157
Printer. *See* Windows printer
Printer properties   150
  Application printing   155
Printers folder   146
  Add printer   147–149
  Delete printer   164
  Generic text printer   160–161
  Network printer   152–153
Program Files   29
Program groups   33
Protocols   167

Quick Launch bar   10, 27, 37, 106
QuickEdit   139

Recent Documents   32
Recycle Bin   27, 30, 32
Regional settings   23, 124
    Date/time   50
    Keyboard   17
    Locale   17
    Time zone   18
Run   30, 96, 102

Save operations   35
Scalability   9
Screensavers   114–115
Search   30–31
Second processor   11
Security
    Certificate   185
    Network   167
    Remembering passwords   75
    Trusted supplier   185
Send To
    Destination   43
    Folder   43
Sharing information   126
Show Desktop   37
Show files   29
ShowSounds   47
Solitaire   65

Sound Recorder   63
SoundSentry   47
Start menu   10, 22, 55, 118–119
    Accessibility   33
    Accessories   33
    Adding My Computer   120
    Folders   33
    Programs   99, 104
    Settings   30
Starting programs   34–35
StickyKeys   47
Summer time   18
System Information
    OLE registration   144
System Tray   27, 37

Taskbar   10, 37
    Customising   121
    Stop program   35
    Switch programs   35
    Toolbars   122–123
Text
    Pasting   130–131
Thumbnails
    In folders   11
    In Paint   60
Time zone   18
ToggleKeys   47

UNC. See Universal Naming Convention
Universal Naming Convention   152
Universal Resource Locator   81, 126
Universal Serial Bus   48
Upgrading your PC   20–21
URL. See Universal Resource Locator
USB. See Universal Serial Bus

Visio 94–95
Volume Control 37, 63

Wallpaper 60
Websites
  Accessibility 47
  Black Box 172
  MSN 81
  Pipex 81
  Upgrade 12
  Windows Update 185–186
Wildcards 31
Win key 31
Windows 2000
  Advanced Server 9
  Components
    Adding/removing 49
  Datacenter Server 9
  Family 8–9
  Games 64–65
  Installing 13–24
  Licences 12
  Performance 11
  Professional 8, 10–11
  Reopening folders at bootup 27
  Repairing 15
  Requirements 13
  Server 8
  Shutdown 38
    Disconnect 38
    Hibernate 38
    Logoff 38
    Restart 38
    Stand by 38
    Upgrade 12
Windows 98 8, 10–11, 15, 20, 49

Windows Explorer 31, 37, 39, 46, 66,
Windows Media Player 62
Windows NT 10–11, 20, 49, 88–90, 106, 154
Windows printer 146
  Add new printer 147–149, 160
  Application printing 155
  Delete 164
  Device settings 150
  Different modes 163
  Document printing 158–159
  Drivers 148
    Other operating system 153
    Verification 154
  Generic text printer 160–161
  Local or network 147
  Manual install 148–149
  Multiple definitions 151
  Network printer 152–153
  Properties 150–151
  Print and hold 162
  Print preview 155
  Print queue 156–157
  Print spooler 156–157
  Printer-ready file 155
  Printers folder 149
  Replacing 164
  Settings 159
Windows Update 26, 30, 49, 68
  Website 185–186
Winnt 19
Wizards
  Add Network Places 10
  Setup 17
WordPad 34, 59, 61, 127, 130–135, 137–138,
    142, 144
Write 61